Hidden in Plain View:
Recognizing the Obvious—
Exploiting the Obscure in Fly Fishing

by Duane Redford

© Copyright 2017 Duane Redford

Cover photo courtesy of Alan Peak

ISBN 978-1-63393-558-7

All rights reserved. No part of this publication may be reproduced, stored in a retrieval system, or transmitted in any form or by any means—electronic, mechanical, photocopy, recording, or any other—except for brief quotations in printed reviews, without the prior written permission of the author.

Published by

Duane Redford
Hidden in Plain View 1st Edition
The Fly Fishers Playbook 1st and 2nd Editions
303.868.2524
https://duaneredford.com/
Fly Designer—Montana Fly Company
Master Nymph Fly Rods Ambassador
@flyfishersplaybook
Follow on Facebook!
Fear No Water

Hidden in Plain View

Recognizing the Obvious—Exploiting the Obscure in Fly Fishing

DUANE REDFORD

Table of Contents

Can You Spot the Fish?. 3

Introduction 5

1. The Journey 9

2. Your Quarter Mile. 19

3. Automatically, Systematically. 32

4. Fly Fishing Formula. 68

5. That's Fly 93

6. You're Soaking in It. 134

7. Wanna Get Better Fast? 155

8. The Dance .187

9. The End or The Beginning. 211

Can You Spot the Fish? (Answer) 214

Acknowledgments. 218

Photo by Tucker Bamford

Can you spot the fish?

see answer on pg. 214

Introduction

WHEN IT COMES to fly fishing, if you're waiting on perfection, you're going to be waiting a long time. Fly fishing is like golf: you don't win it, you play it. You participate in hopes that you continually get better. Each time out becomes an opportunity to learn and improve. You can improve everything from casting to reading the water and the insect identification each time your boots get wet. The goal is to become proficient, better than proficient really, and the best way to accomplish this goal is to spend time on the river. Quality time.

I have been toting a fly rod for the better part of four decades. I've been blessed to fly fish many beautiful places. I feel as if I have always walked away from the river better than when I started. I want to improve every time out. As a former college baseball player, and high school baseball and football coach of many, many years, I tried to instill the same thoughts in my players. Be better today than you were yesterday. Find something to improve in your game through each experience, regardless if it's practice or a game. Each and every experience becomes a bona–fide learning experience, an opportunity to improve.

Experience has always been the best teacher; however, if you keep making the same mistakes, that mitigates the benefits. All you end up doing is reinforcing bad habits. I began playing baseball at the age of six, and continued through college. I remember going through hitting slumps from time to time. I would jump into the batting cage and hit until my hands bled. Unfortunately, in most cases, I was simply reinforcing bad habits that caused the slump in the first place. Furthermore, I was developing brand–new lousy habits at the same time. How in the world do you overcome that cycle?

After going through it countless times, it's my opinion that the best way to overcome a slump is by going back to the basics, recognizing the obvious, and exploiting the obscure. Sometimes this takes a qualified eye watching what you are doing from a distance; sometimes you can pull yourself out of the abyss. Either way, it takes a conscious effort.

If you're new to the sport of fly fishing and you are not catching fish, you're probably not capturing the basics of the sport. It might be your drift, it might be failure to recognize a fish eating your offering, or maybe you're not drifting the correct offerings at the correct speed and depths. There are certainly other factors that may be hindering your success, but typically, beginners suffer from those basic maladies.

How do you get out of that slump? Read everything you can, watch others do it properly, find a qualified eye to observe you, and fish, fish, fish. In other words, learn to recognize the obvious.

The obvious is what experienced fly fishers already know and take for granted. They are further down the road on the way to perfection. They see and adjust for conditions that are readily obvious for their skill level. They just know. The sooner you learn to recognize the obvious and "just know," the sooner you can advance to the next level, which includes the ability to exploit the obscure. More on the obscurities in fly fishing later.

The next level I will refer to is that of the intermediate angler. This angler knows the basic fundamentals of the cast, the drift, and "fish take" recognition, but aren't at the stage where they can recognize the obscurities of the sport. There are still holes in their game, but they can move fish. Most often, they don't know what they don't know, but their limited success keeps them hungry and coming back for more.

How does an intermediate angler battle a slump? By going back to the basics. Unlike the beginner, an intermediate has basic fundamentals to fall back on. These fundamentals may be less than desired or not perfectly aligned for quick progress, but the angler has enough skill to catch fish on their own. If a beginner is struggling with a nymph rig roll cast, a demonstration may be in order, but an intermediate angler only needs to be reminded of rod tip placement and paying attention to the rod tip path to get out of their roll-casting slump.

Let's take a look at what makes advanced anglers advanced. These guys and gals have all the fundamentals, characteristics, and mechanics figured out. They may still be mastering a specific skill, but these folks can flat-out fish. It takes a long time to get to this level and there is always more to learn or perfect, but that's the nature of the fly fishing beast. It's a game we play.

How does an advanced angler battle a slump? Generally, they battle slumps by exploiting the obscure. They have seen many things, and battled many conditions on many bodies of water. The experience level of some of these folks is legendary. I remember asking an old-timer once from across the river what he caught his last fish on. He looked at me wryly and shouted over the sound of the water, "Experience!" Not sure who got the bigger kick out of his reply, him or me.

Advanced anglers know how to fool fish, how to stay ahead of the hatch, and how to get a deeper understanding of fly fishing success. Let's say an advanced angler is nymphing a run, and is not hooking as many fish as usual. To him it's a slump, although most people would be satisfied with number of hook-ups. Capitalizing on what the river is giving obviously is easy, but there is something missing for this angler and he knows it. To overcome this slump, the advanced angler draws on knowledge and experience, and begins to examine where within the nymph drift he is getting hook–ups. This obscure tidbit will give him enough information to make many mini–adjustments to his rig, to exploit what most don't even recognize.

This book is designed to help the beginner to recognize what long–timers call the obvious, intermediates to begin the ascent into advanced level, and advanced anglers to take that last step into looking at the river differently than before.

I have stood with clients on the bridge off Highway 6 in Wolcott, Colorado, and watched men from many countries fish the Eagle River for the World Championships. The World Fly Fishing Championships pit elite competitors from twenty–seven countries against one another in a seven–day fly fishing event. These folks are the best of the best when it comes to catching fish on the fly. I always tell my clients to just observe and then tell me what they see. Every time I have had a client say something along the lines of "I would have never thought to fish that piece of water; how in the heck did he know there was a fish in there?"

I usually reply, "Yep, they are fishing where others won't because most don't recognize it as feeding water. That guy is simply exploiting the obscure."

The Journey

"IF I WANT to go for a hike, I'd bring my dog, not my fly rod." Those were the exact words a client relayed to me not too long ago. He was referring to the experience of a guided fly–fishing trip. He's there for the total experience, but also wants to catch fish. Some would scoff at his attitude, saying that he has his priorities jumbled, because the real reason to fly fish is for the experience of simply being in or a part of nature. I disagree. Why carry a fly rod if you don't wish to catch fish?

Let's imagine I take you to home plate at a major league baseball stadium armed with a bat, a bucket of baseballs, and a tee. I set the tee on the plate, tee up a ball, put the bat in your hands and walk away exclaiming, "I'll be back in a half hour." What would you do? It's a fair bet that most if not all of you would look over your shoulder to see if anyone is watching, and then you would attempt to hit the ball off the tee. Sure, you'd soak in the smell of the dirt and grass, be awestruck by the size of the stadium, and marvel at the sound of bat against ball, but you'd be there to hit the ball off the tee.

I think it's also safe to surmise that you would reach into the bucket, tee up another, and try to hit it better than the last one. Then you would begin to think about your swing, and make a few technical changes to hit the ball more squarely. Before you knew it, you'd be trying to place the ball in certain places in the field, and maybe even go so far as to see how far you could hit it. You'd be making physical adjustments to hit the ball with more authority and control. You'd probably empty the ball bucket before I returned.

Same goes for fly fishing. You're there, fly rod in hand, standing shin–deep in the drink. Although you may be soaking up the sights and sounds of nature, you're going to try to catch a few. That's why we fly fish; we are there to catch fish. Some folks have more drive, maybe a somewhat unhealthy drive, to catch fish. Others are content with a few. Yes, it's about the experience, but isn't it great when you hook fish on a fly rod and hit it out of the park?

You see, you're not waiting on perfection while fly fishing: you're striving for it. We are anxious to make even the slightest of adjustments to our rigs, rods, and presentations to catch more fish, all the while standing in a place where we are soaking up the area with our senses. My contention is simple: anglers are there to catch fish. Some are more focused than others, but that is the primary goal, to catch as many as possible while soaking in nature. I am not professing keeping count of the fish you catch on a fly rod. To the contrary, I always tell my clients that if they need to keep a count, they should count how many good drifts they can make consecutively. The fish numbers magically go up when they actively dial in their drift mechanics, instead of just looking to hook as many as possible.

That same client told me later, "It sure is beautiful out here today, even nicer since I'm hooking a few."

"Yep," I replied. "I get it, so do you."

Relax

Among all the statistics I keep from year to year regarding what the fish, bugs, and weather are doing every day, I wish I would remember to keep records of a phenomenon that I see happen too often to count. It's uncanny how many times that just after I walk away from a client, he or she hooks up on a fish. I used to think it was an odd coincidence, but over the years I've begun to figure out why it really happens. I am convinced folks hook up on fish after I leave their side simply because they relax.

Folks tend to tense up when I'm standing next to them. Clients that have fished with me realize I am as calm as they come, I try to work on one skill at a time, I don't bark orders unless we're fighting a fish, and I relish every second of doing what we're doing, so I don't feel as if I'm too intimidating. However, I recently had the good fortune to head to Alaska to do a bit of fishing. That first day with a guide standing next to me was a bit daunting, and I began to realize there would be inherent pressure even if he wasn't saying anything.

Ever sit facing a computer screen with someone looking over your shoulder trying to point something out to you? How hard does it become to see what they're pointing out? How's that for anxiety? It becomes nearly impossible to find what you're looking for, even though you know it's right in front of you, and the pressure is nearly paralyzing at times. Same holds true for fly fishing. I call this FWI or Fishing While Impaired, and it should be illegal in every state. Whether we realize it or not, there's always a bit of anxiety when doing any type of fishing. We're there for a reason, right? It's inherent in the endeavor. There's at least a modicum of anxiety when you begin the pursuit.

**Relaxing and observing makes the experience so much more rewarding.
Photo courtesy Bob Streb**

Fly fishing is one of those endeavors that gets better the more you relax. The simple fact that someone is in your space, someone you may really want to please, makes the anxiety levels rise and the experience turns counterproductive. An old college baseball coach of mine used to bark, "Anxiety is the shortcut to failure. Relax or I'm gonna run y'all!" Because of the threat of making us run cross-country, that didn't really work the way he thought it would, and our anxiety actually increased more often than not. When fly fishing, once you begin to relax, absorb the cadence of the river, and control the mechanics of the cast, drift, and set without *being* mechanical, that's when you become your most productive. The ability to relax when fly fishing is one of those obscure tools that we all need to find room for in our fly box.

You're going to fail more than you succeed in fly fishing. Like in baseball, you can still get to the Hall of Fame being successful three out of ten times over your career. When nymphing, you probably only hook fifty percent of the fish that you actually witness moving your indicator, and you may only land half of those. Those numbers are probably a bit on the high side for the average angler, so suffice it to say, we're leaving a lot of fish that ate, unmolested. You're going to fail in fly fishing. Just learn how to fail fast, get right back in the water, and work on improving your skills.

Drowning in Information

I've said many times that fly fishing is a lot like golf: you don't really win it, you play it, you participate. Sure, you're competing, but some get confused about with whom they're competing. I contend that even if you're a member of a world team competing for a championship, you're really competing with Mama Nature. She will decide the eventual winners and losers. It's always been that way. Mama Nature has the last word, so you might as well play along and try to learn as much as possible about how to maximize your chances at catching fish.

Everywhere you look, there's material you can find that gives fly fishing information. It's one of those endeavors where we are drowning in information but starving for knowledge. We are inundated with how-tos, equipment reviews, and opinions, but many don't really have the missing ingredient: the experience to make it all fit.

I remember as a kid, probably fifteen years old or so, yelling up stream at the Firehole River in Montana to my dad, "What'd you catch that one on?"

He yelled back, "A good drift!" In other words, *Figure it out, kid.*

There's the written and digitized information, and the information that comes from experience. The experience derived from doing or watching others do. The experience that comes from attempting to apply what you've seen and read and tried on your own. You fail or succeed and you learn from it. Your common sense and ability to rationalize why you failed or succeeded, coupled with learning to avoid failure and foster success, lead to knowledge.

Information is simply data, while knowledge makes that data useful. You have to analyze to get knowledge; to get information, you just observe. Here's the kicker: all that knowledge you've been gathering is useless without experience. In other words, go fish. Go fish a lot.

Why am I carrying on so about knowledge, information, and experience? I'm carrying on because fly fishing is a long journey down a short road. Modest proficiency can occur quickly in your journey; however, the last few miles on the path to excellence can take years. Look at the journey as a road ten miles long. Most folks don't take too long to get to mile marker five. Mile marker seven takes an incredible amount of "water time" accumulated, and mile marker ten, in my mind, is perfection. If I were to scout myself like a major league scout scores a player, I'd honestly put myself in the mile–marker–seven–to–seven–and–a–half range. I'm good enough to put hundreds of people on fish a year, write a few books on the subject, and travel the country speaking to many different groups, clubs, and organizations, but I don't know what I don't yet know about fly fishing. The bad news is I need more work; the good news is I need more water time to get to the next levels.

Janet Redford is enjoying the journey of fly fishing and quickly becoming proficient.

I am trying to move beyond knowledge and experience. I want more. I want fly fishing wisdom. I have heard people say that good judgment comes from experience, and experience comes from bad judgment. I want the ability to improve on my experience, good or bad, my knowledge, and my judgment. I want to develop the kind of judgment that displays the powers of reasoning, and is grounded in perceptions, shrewdness, acumen, and logic. Then it becomes natural to see, give thought to, and understand things on the river that others do not: the ability to recognize the obvious, and exploit the obscure.

Recognizing the Obvious

I am blessed to be able to travel this country and give presentations on fly fishing. One of my latest presentations had a slide that was a picture of a very famous candy bar sitting on a table. As the slide opened, I would ask who knew which type of candy bar it was. Invariably, every hand would rise (I think they thought the first to answer would get the candy bar). Most folks would recognize and name it quickly. Then, I would open a slide showing a familiar shape of a candy bar, but it was impossible to tell which kind it was. It could have caramel, peanuts, whatever, but you wouldn't be able to tell until you opened it what was really inside. Hands would still shoot up, but there weren't nearly as many, and the guesses were mostly comical.

It's easy to recognize the obvious, and we anglers are a confident bunch when we are sure of what lies ahead. Just like the candy bar, when you know what's in the river in front of you, how to read it, and how to fish it, you beam with confidence. We are not nearly as confident when we are unsure or unfamiliar with what lies ahead and it's not so easy to read.

There is a process that can help recognize the obvious, and we will cover it in this book. It's what the 10 percent that are catching fish learned many water days ago. They systematically cover the water without consciously thinking about it. It's what my dad meant when he said he caught that fish with a good drift. I didn't understand then, because I didn't yet see the river the same as he. His prowess in recognizing what the river and fish were giving him allowed him to exploit what he recognized.

Exploiting the Obscure

I have often heard it said that 10 percent of your fly fishers catch 90 percent of the fish. I have to say, I find that to be fairly accurate, especially during days when the fishing is, for whatever reason, more difficult. I have witnessed more than a handful of situations where one or two anglers are moving many more fish than everyone else. Not too long ago, I watched as two guys in float tubes caught several fish to everyone else's few on a crowded mountain lake in Arizona. These guys were intermixed with the other float tubers and had it dialed in. Even floating in my tube, with my back turned to them, I could hear that telltale sound of rods lifting and lines ripping off the surface. No whooping or hollering, just a calm confidence that comes with kicking everyone's ass. At least they offered me a few flies . . .

What did they see that others didn't? Through knowledge acquired from experience, these folks have figured out the nuances and obscurities others don't readily notice. They recognize the minute details in structure, fish, and insect behaviors, and exploit what Mama Nature throws at them regarding environmental, historical, and seasonal conditions.

Take a look at the brook trout pictured on the next page. It's obvious it's a big brookie. What's not so obvious at first glance is that it has a snake running the length of its body and then some. I enjoy showing folks this picture. Some see the snake right off, and some have to be given a few clues as to what they're seeing. The snake is there, but we aren't programmed to recognize a snake going into and out of a fish. Then, once you figure out what you're looking at, your mind automatically connects the snake. That's the hidden in plain view part. The premise of this book is that once you see or do something in the fly fishing world, it's no longer obscure, but begins to become obvious. If I put this same picture on the last page, you'd recognize it immediately.

From obscure to obvious. This Brookie was hooked after it took a streamer.
Courtesy Joel B. Sharp

It doesn't stop there, however. They also fish with a confidence that comes from years of trial and error (mostly error), and techniques that often match the obscurity that most of us miss. These are the folks that cast proficiently, mend fantastically, read what most of us don't even see in a run, and, even if they are using the wrong flies, will catch more fish than the rest of us.

I get to stand in a river and watch folks fish. I really enjoy taking a peek at the scenery now and then as I go about my job. One of my favorite things to observe are the many swallows that cruise the Eagle River in Colorado. It's neat because they're usually consuming a fine hatch of baetis, pale morning duns (PMD's), or caddis, but it is also neat to watch behaviors of individual swallows. There are always one or two that are flat–out consuming more than the rest of the flock. Are they better fliers than the rest? Do they have more chicks than the others back in the mud hut on the bridge? Well, barring injury or other impairments for those birds that make up the rest of the flock, I'd surmise that those one or two birds that I witness eating more bugs just want it more. They're hungrier and they combine technique, skill, and confidence to eat many more bugs than the rest.

Same holds true for those that consistently out fish the rest of us. They also combine technique, skill, and confidence to move dozens more fish than the mere mortal. They are the ten–percenters, and they are just as content sitting on the bank waiting for that one fish to rise as they are trying something out of their "program" like swinging wet flies all day. In other words, they get it, in more ways than one.

So sit back and settle in. We're about to start digging into their world. It's hidden in plain view.

Your Quarter Mile

BEFORE WE CAN go another step, we need to have a common language. I tend to define things differently than most folks, so in order to figure out how the ten–percenters exploit obscurities, we have to be able to define and recognize the obvious when it comes to fly fishing in general. That comes with the need to have a common language: to speak the same terms and examine things through a common lens. We'll call the common lens the quarter mile, and we will use it to not only gain a common language and a common perspective, but begin to show distinctly obvious components and characteristics, and how to search them out.

The quarter mile of river is a simple, metaphorical term for characteristics of a river we can define in a manageable section or portion of a river. In other words, a section of river that has many different features that can be readily defined, named, and recognized, with a consistent naming convention. It doesn't need to be a quarter mile long, and although continuity would be nice, it doesn't have to be continuous. Again, it is to our advantage to have a consistent language to move forward in this pursuit, and it is also advantageous for the early–stage angler to have a river to call home.

Most rivers possess common characteristics, with one major difference being how steep or how much grade a river has. Some rivers drop more quickly than others, adding additional speed to their personalities. Others flow slowly along flatter surfaces. Some rivers are freestones, that is to say undammed rivers; others are tailwaters, emanating from the reservoir behind a dam. Some wind hairpin after hairpin through the plains, while others rush headlong through boulder–strewn valleys. Keep in mind, however, that you can still find many commonalities between these types of rivers, although one may have to look harder in a few instances.

Folks ask me a lot how they can become better fly fishers quickly. I always explain that they need to find their own quarter mile of river, or home river, and fish it all four seasons. When selecting your quarter mile, look for as much personality and river character as possible. The more character, the better, because this forces you to learn several skills to master your selected section while you master the obvious and begin to recognize the obscurities. Look for a section that has at least five of the following characteristics:

- Riffle Section: 6" to 30" deep of faster "textured water" before a shelf.
- Shelf: Drop directly after a riffle section. May be gradual or abrupt. Can be across or along the river bottom. Look for a shelf section 3 to 10 feet long if possible.
- Pool Section: Directly connected to the shelf after full depth has been achieved.
- Tailout Section: End of the pool section as it begins to flatten out and become shallow before the next riffle section.
- Bend: Where the river changes direction by more than 15 degrees.

- Island Seam: Where two or more braids from the main stem of the river join, at the end or tip of the downstream side of the island.
- Bars: Elevated areas of flow-deposited material (mud, sand, gravel, etc.). Bars can be located at the mouth of a river. Middle channels are often found on inside edges of a river and are sometimes called longitudinal shelves or point bars.
- Eddies: Water that is generally flowing in the opposite direction of the river. Usually found behind large obstructions or at the edges of a river. Easily identifiable, especially when you fish them.
- Pockets: Where several boulders are randomly placed in the main stem, creating fish holds and insect superhighways through horizontal and vertical compression of the water.
- Sweepers: Large logs or brush piles positioned to funnel water flows and insects to holding fish.
- Glide: Elongated shallow extension of the pool prior to the tailout. Depths are generally two and a half to four feet (some exceptions occur), and flows are walking speed or less until you near the tailout and the glide picks up pace.

The list above explains the obvious river characteristics common to most streams. An angler's mission should be to learn and understand those components so well that he or she can predict where the fish will be holding and why. The goal is to eventually learn to exploit that which isn't so obvious. These obscurities lie within the characteristics outlined above, and the more you learn the obvious, the more the obscurities become clear. So your quarter mile of river should have at least five of the above characteristics in an obvious way. I will guarantee you that if it does, you'll find another five characteristics at a minimum that are obscure and need exploitation. Just like there's a fish in front of every rock, there are obscurities in every run.

Here's a typical run on the Poudre river. The transitions are easily identified and assist in determining a common language. The river is flowing from the bottom right to the top left in this picture.

In looking at the picture, above, of what I deem a typical run, you can see the riffle that begins the run, the shelf area, the less textured pool area, the tailout, and finally the next riffle. A run defined this way is easy to read, because you are simply searching for the first and last riffles. A run can have short or long sections.

My favorite run to guide on the Eagle River is down by the town of Gypsum. There's a long, straight, and flat section that precedes it, and it makes a slight right bend as it forms the riffle section. The riffle section is maybe thirty feet long maximum. Even in high water, it is only about eighteen inches deep. The riffle gives way to a shelf section that perfectly bisects the bend all the way across. The shelf length is less than six feet and drops vertically about three feet.

There are perfectly placed boulders ranging from bowling–ball to laundry–basket size through the pool section that is a mere fifty feet long before it tails out into the next riffle. The entire run (as I define it) is about forty–five steps in length and fifty steps across. I've watched countless people walk right on by as they fish the river. As of this writing I have yet to put clients in there that haven't hooked fish. What are those who pass it missing, other than the fish?

That run has nearly everything I'm after as a fly fisher reading water. Cold, oxygenated water from a concentrated shelf section that gives way to an abrupt shelf that perfectly holds feeding fish, soft inside and outside seams that are moving about walking speed, great pool section protection with sleeper seams, and a concise tailout near fast water. As far as water that holds feeding fish, this is one of the best runs I've found, if not the best. It produces year–round in all types of conditions, except for when it's flowing chocolate.

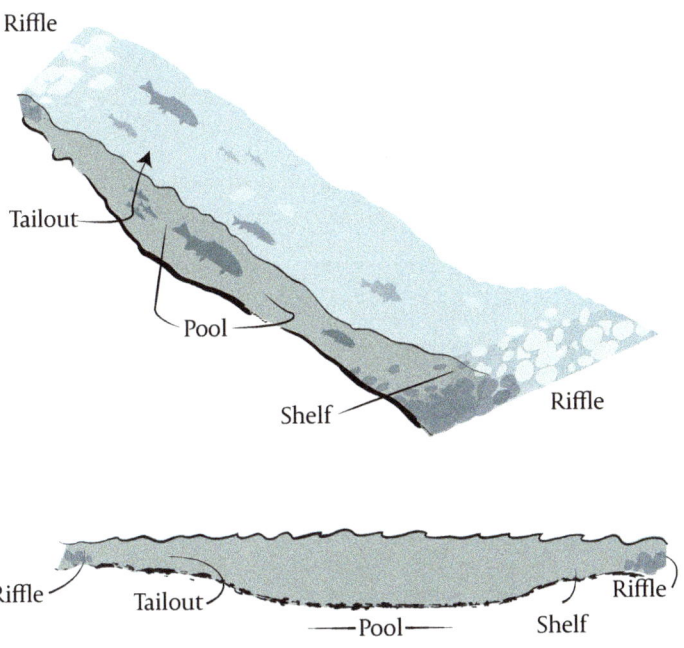

This is an isometric and a cross-sectional view of a typical run. The water is flowing from the riffle-to shelf-to pool-to tailout- to riffle. Quick identification of these run components is important to your success.

Stats Don't Lie

When I was coaching baseball. I relied on statistics to assist in making decisions. With the aid of "stats", I could comfortably make decisions based on large quantities of numerical data. Armed with this data I felt comfortable drawing conclusions and making decisions based on probability. Stats don't lie in baseball, they don't lie in fly fishing either. This past year alone, I've compiled, with the help of colleague and friend Levi Lambert, nearly four hundred hours of on-river observations. We studied everything from weather to insects to fish behavior, with tons of information in between. For purposes of this discussion, we will focus on a few of the highlights.

Here are a few observations, based in fact, made this past season. They comply with the statistical observations from the last three years as well, so we're looking at a full four years of statistical observations from the river. Most of the fish hooked were in seams eighteen to thirty inches of water. The speed of that water was roughly walking speed, and it is adjacent to either deeper or faster water. In other words, the fish were eating while in seams less than three feet deep that were also right next to deeper or faster water for safety escape routes. This type of seam is very easily located, and it's obvious that if and when fish move into this seam, they are there to feed.

Most fish were hooked on the shelf section of the run. The larger fish were hooked in the tailouts. A full 64 percent of the fish hooked, landed, and documented were collected on the shelf as we define it. That is astounding. It makes perfect sense, though, because that's where the water is richest in bugs and oxygen. In most cases, it's very fish-safe, because not only are the fish adjacent to a riffle or a pool, but the water is typically not at its shallowest here, which offers them even more safety. Remember, this water is also cruising along at about walking speed and is up to about three feet deep.

Are you starting to get the point? Might not be a bad idea to re-read that last paragraph: it's really loaded with important information. When you're in search of your quarter mile, you should now have a bit more information to help narrow your search. It's out there, and some of you are smiling because you already know where.

Why all the big fish in the tailouts? Let's further define a tailout. It's typically the section just before the next set of riffles, immediately after the pool section. The water begins to become shallower. In many cases it also picks up pace, character, and texture. It is still in between deeper or faster water for safety. Big fish dig it. My theory on why big fish hold there is simple: most folks walk right by the tailout because they either don't recognize it or don't know how to fish it. Maybe a combination of both.

If I'm a big, dominant fish looking for a place that is bug–rich because the water is compressing or getting shallower and thus becoming more saturated with insects, *and* folks tend to leave me alone in my prime lie, I'm going to set up shop in the tailout until I'm forcibly moved. A full 47 percent of fish sixteen inches in length and longer have come from the tailouts, according to my statistics. That's a huge number compared to 16 percent coming from the pool and glide section, and 36 percent coming from the shelf, and offers further proof that big fish aren't stupid. We are going to cover techniques to get after these fish in subsequent chapters. Oh, and while you're thinking about it, remember to add a good tailout to your quarter–mile selection.

Levi Lambert with a beauty he hooked while nymphing the tailout of the run in the background. Photo courtesy Levi Lambert

It's clear that most of the best hook rates come from the top and bottoms of a run, but let's not discount some other special holding areas in a typical run. After the riffles cascade over the shelf section, the water dumps into the pool section. The pool section typically is moving slower than the rest of the run, but still may have seams along the edges and in various locations that hold feeding fish. My statistics show that I catch more than a handful in the pool section, but usually closer to the shelf than the tailout and typically on the outside or inside of the pool as it nears the bank. I have found that as the water begins to slow in the pool, most fish inhabiting it are not actively feeding. I say most fish, but fish are live creatures and sometimes break the mold and lazily feed in these sections.

Most pool sections where I guide and fish are between three and five feet deep, and the closer you are to the middle of the pool, the slower it moves. The key is finding the section of the pool that has character. Typically, the texture of the waters' surface will give you several clues as to what's going on subsurface. For example, you may see a triangular disturbance facing downstream in a pool section, or a longitudinal seam forming a foam line. Both of those examples clearly depict that something is going on subsurface, and they should be investigated, because they may hold feeding fish. If you can see fish in the pool, stealthily observe them, and try to ascertain if they are feeding or holding. If they are simply holding, note their positions and keep an eye on them. Ofttimes, those holding fish will move up into the shelf area and begin to feed. Move up with them.

On the Eagle River, there are several runs that have long shallow pool sections. They are easy to identify because the depth is fairly consistent and usually between two and a half and four feet. When I see a long pool section such as this, I call it a glide. Glides can be very productive, especially when there is good structure subsurface and deeper or faster water along at least one edge. Glides are especially fun when conditions are ripe for dry fly action or anytime you want to swing streamers. Usually, this takes advanced angling skills in casting and mending, because glides can be difficult to wade, and longer casts may be necessary to avoid spooking fish. Glides also afford feeding fish a chance to really look over your offering, so mending for drift speed, mending while not over fish, and proper leader and tippet lengths and sizes are very important. If you're floating glides where fish are feeding, you can have stellar days.

My statistics rank glides as very productive during solid blue–winged olive (BWO), pale morning dun (PMD), and caddis hatches where dry fly and dry dropper rigs can be utilized, but they are not nearly as productive as shelves and tailouts when conditions call for only nymphing. The slow, shallow water is difficult to nymph for most because of the complex mechanics of the drift and trouble presenting multi-fly and indicator rigs stealthily to exposed fish. You can combat these difficulties by looking for seams along the edges or subsurface obstructions throughout the glide. There are other tactics for this area we will discuss at length later.

Seams are formed anytime you have two different speeds of water running parallel to one another. Seams hold fish for the reasons I have outlined, and rank very high with all methods of take, year-round. Again, the most productive seams are walking speed, 18–30 inches in depth and right next to safety water. Usually you can find great action in seams created by an island point. The beauty of island points is you can usually fish them year-round, even in runoff high water, because the island creates one big obstruction, and the island point represents two bug-rich seams converging into one in feeding-fish-friendly water. Island points can be fantastic in high-water conditions because of the way they slow down the river and protect fish from the harshness of water speed, if you can get to them safely.

One of my favorite island seams is on the Miracle Mile, on the North Platte River between the Seminole and Pathfinder Reservoirs. It sits in the perfect position for high water because the island is situated close to one of the exterior banks of the main stem of the river. This makes it fairly easy to reach from the shore in high water, and you can quickly traverse down the island to the point and hook feeding fish. On more than one occasion, I've locked arms with a buddy or two to cross the narrow seam and get to the goods.

If you can locate it on a river you fish, look for an island point that connects to a shelf. I have found several over the years and all have been productive. There is one on a river I used to guide: if I needed a fish, I would make my way there. An island point connected to a shelf is an excellent spot for locating feeding fish simply because it represents several characteristics that point to safe fish feeding behaviors. The key to finding fish consistently is to try to combine the most productive aspects of a run. Okay, so, island points to shelves are good. What about riffles to shelves in a bend section? Or what about a shelf to a bar with an eddy under foam? That's the idea: learn every part of a run. Call it what you wish and try to combine as many outstanding features as possible within your quarter mile.

So let's talk about the shelf to a bar with an eddy under foam. Sounds intriguing, right? A bar is usually a rock or sand structure that slowly gains depth from the river edge toward the middle. It's a longitudinal shelf of sorts and can occur from inside edges to mid-channel. Combine the longitudinal shelf with a shelf that crosses the river perpendicularly, and you have double the pleasure. Two shelf sections, preceded by a riffle that has an adjacent eddy under foam? Too much? Not if you approach it systematically and incrementally, instead of trying to fish the beast all at once. Slow down, break it down, and attack it piece by piece.

Selection Made Simple

Although it's desirable to be continuous or connected, your quarter mile doesn't necessarily have to be. It may prove a bit of a challenge to find several obvious river characteristics I've listed in a neat package, all connected. However, when selecting your quarter mile's characteristics, try to keep them as close as possible, because of a few variables that can substantially affect how your selection fishes.

When making your selection, attempt to prevent any tributaries flowing between your selected features. Tributaries can substantially affect water clarity and water temperatures during different times of the year. I know of several tributaries that will blow out the river downstream of them during snow melt or thunderstorm runoff. While the runoff effects can be obvious when it comes to river clarity, temperature variations are not always as obvious. Both situations can hamper the fish's willingness to feed and the insect hatches.

Be mindful of any type of power plants or other industries that collect river water as a part of their processing and eventually dump the water back into the main stem of the river. I know of a few places on the Eagle River that have this problem. Although they can be beneficial in the winter and early spring where a couple-degree spike up in the river can spur fish into eating, they have an adverse effect in the dog days of summer. High water temperatures put a cap on fish eagerness and catching and landing fish safely.

Waters that emanate from behind a dam, or tailwaters, usually have more consistent flows and temperatures. Although hatches can be more sporadic than freestone rivers, and not quite as prolific in sheer numbers, they are generally more consistent. It is usually easier to locate your quarter mile on a tailwater than on a "wild," undammed freestone river, simply because there aren't as many variables, due to the metered water flows. Still, watch out for tributaries and springs.

Familiar and Unfamiliar Water

Why all the hubbub when it comes to selecting your quarter mile? Simply put, you want to find the most consistent characteristics you can. The more consistent your selections, the faster you can learn. If you are questioning conditions that you can't control, such as differences in hatches, flows, and temperatures, then you are spending less time reading water and effectively fishing. Doubt is the great destroyer in fly fishing. Confidence is key. Even if you didn't do well on your quarter mile today, you can eliminate most factors out of your control and walk away knowing you fished it better than last time.

It won't take you very long to become proficient on your quarter mile. Fish it a handful of times, especially if you're catching fish, and you'll gain proficiency and confidence in no time. That comes back to the experience and knowledge argument. Fish more for experience and fish well for knowledge. In no time at all, you'll be able to read that water quickly and astutely in various conditions. You'll begin to get ahead of the hatch, and not only anticipate what flies to rig and throw, but systematically approach bug selection and where your next cast, drift, and mend will be. Factors such as off-color tributary flows and affected water temperatures won't be a big deal as you progress to the next levels with confidence.

Here's the beauty of this method: once you've gained confidence, you then can begin to apply what you've learned to the rest of the river you have chosen, and most any river where you can wet your waders. At this point in my guiding career, I actually like to take clients to water that I've never laid eyes on. It's exciting to read the water quickly for content and apply all that I have learned as I fish it through my clients.

Recognizing typical run components can be mastered fairly quickly if you break it down to your quarter mile and fish it often, and as you become proficient you can begin to locate and master other obvious components. Recognizing the components of a run is one thing, learning to fish them effectively is another. We are going to dig into the obvious run characteristics one by one, and discuss the best methods to attack each component. As we dig through that information, we will also begin to look at the more obscure. There's more that we don't see than we do see. Furthermore, the more run characteristics you learn to recognize quickly, the more obscurities you'll be able to exploit.

Automatically, Systematically

YEARS AGO—BUT I remember this as if it was yesterday—I had crossed a section of the South Platte near Deckers, Colorado, and was waiting for my two clients to catch up. Well, they were taking their sweet time, so I did what I usually do, and started poking around the laundry basket–sized rocks I was standing amongst. Eventually I spied a fairly large dead spider, legs sucked in around its body as they're inclined to, laying in a narrow split in a rock. After convincing myself that it was truly dead, I plucked it out of the crack with two fingers. My plan was to scare one of my clients by throwing it at him, but he was still standing mid–river, talking with his buddy. After waiting a bit, losing interest in scaring him and wanting to get this dead critter out of my hand, I decided to watch it float downstream, so I found a soft side current and prepared to set it free.

Something made me change my mind about floating it on the surface, so I decided to put it about a foot below the surface and observe how the water's current affected it. Once in position under the water's surface, I gently released it, making sure it wasn't in my downstream current, but completely off to one side. What I saw surprised me. It changed my thinking about fly selection and drift techniques. That spider turned, fluttered, rose, and dropped at the whim of the tiny currents that carried it. I was sold, and from then on have strived to fish lively bugs in a dead drift.

Redford's Spider Bite. A lively fly in a dead drift pattern is deadly effective. Hook-MFC #16 7125, Body-Hareline Tan Dub, Black Razor foam (.5mm) wrap, Head-Black Sparkle Dub wrapped back from eye, Thread-Pink UTC 70.

Up until then, I had fished weighted bugs in the majority of my dry drop and nymph rigs. I got to thinking of how drastically the spider's freedom drift would have been different if he'd been equipped with a tungsten bead. Certainly, you can envision the difference between the two drifts and the impact that may have on feeding fish. I tie my flies weight–free, because I am looking for as close to a lifelike drift as possible. It's perfectly suited to nymphing under an indicator and dry dropper rigs.

You may be wondering, *What about European Nymphing? Those flies are weighted.* That's a logical question that has a logical answer. The Euro crowd fishes without an indicator; they are directly connected to the fly, and have customized rigs and techniques that bring lifelike dead drifts to their flies. Their flies are typically sparse and connected to light tippets; thus, they get quick sink rates and less drag than one would think. On the other hand, I am using an indicator between my fly rod and the flies. This creates a hinge in my leader and a distinct disconnect between flies and rod tip. I'm running flies on heavier tippets (4x typically), and my flies aren't nearly as sparse with legs, foam, and soft hackles coming into play. If I weight the bugs, they don't flow freely under the indicator; instead, they become plow jockeys, barreling and bouncing downstream. I prefer to take advantage of the hinge created, and another hinge that is a bit more obscure, and strive for lively bugs in each dead drift. I want my bugs to drift as closely to the dead spider drift as possible.

Let's talk some more about the merits and downfalls of indicator or suspension rigs and European–style nymphing. I am by no means an expert on European–style nymphing. That said, I have watched many world competitors strut their stuff at the World Fly Fishing Championships on many occasions, read good material on the subject, and watched more than a few how–to videos. I'm by no means accomplished in that style, but I've done it more than a few times, so I think I have a handle on the concept and can do a fair comparison between the two styles.

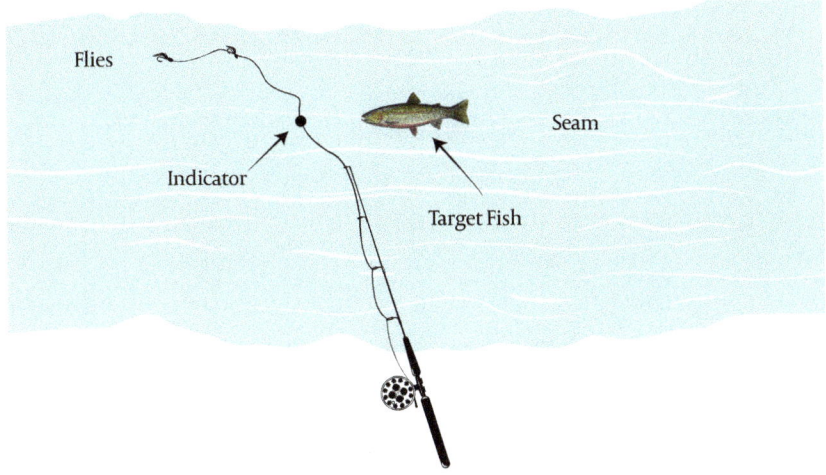

Use special mending skills and casting angles to strive to get your flies and indicator in the same seam as often as possible.

Unlike Euro–style nymphers, who can be pinpoint accurate with the cast and ensuing drift, the indicator fly fisher has difficulty putting the flies and the indicator in the same seam. You have a lot of line below the indicator, and when you cast, your indicator may hit four to five feet this side of your flies. If you don't know what you're doing, you'll complete the entire drift without ever getting your flies and indicator in the same seam. This will usually cause your flies to travel too fast for the seam you're in, and will put most of the fish off. There are a couple of ways to correct this. You can learn how to nymph fish at upstream angles or perfect the ability to pause and release your indicator after the initial cast through stacking and piling mends. There aren't any rules saying you can't adjust where you put your flies or when you "release" the drift after you cast: you do what you need to do to succeed. Look for these techniques in Chapter 8.

Tackling Tackle

In the next diagram, you can see that hinge points are created at the indicator and at the weight in the in-line nymph rig. The hinge created by the indicator is obvious, the hinge created by the weight is obscure. I want as much control over both hinges as I can get. The top hinge, created by the indicator to weight section and a floating fly line, controls the depth of the rig, and can be very versatile in many different scenarios with changes in casting angles and distance. This "upper" hinge controls my overall depth. Calculating it is usually observable. The old rule of setting your indicator to 1½ times the depth of the water is strictly a starting point, and I have found over the years that I toss out this rule and abide by observation, casting angles, and distance. Remember, setting depth usually only requires skill of observation.

Old rules can be questioned, but some old rigging rules are bulletproof and time-tested. The old rule about having tippet and leaders match the conditions present, your tactics, and the fish you're after still holds true. If I'm chasing large trout in a high off-color river, I'll opt for heavier leaders and tippets than if I'm chasing pressured trout in gin clear low water on my favorite tailwater. That's just common sense. I always use a monofilament leader, usually a 7½ foot 4x, and after the rigging is complete, this rig is pushing 9½ feet in total length, which is perfect for the waters I guide and fish pretty much year-round. I like to use 4x fluorocarbon tippet between my flies for most of the year, except when the water conditions dictate. When the water becomes lower and clear, I change to 5x fluorocarbon for additional stealth. The only times I'll switch to a 6x tippet is when I'm dropping a dry off the back of another dry fly, and for my nymph, dry-drop, and dry fly rigs, I always use floating fly line.

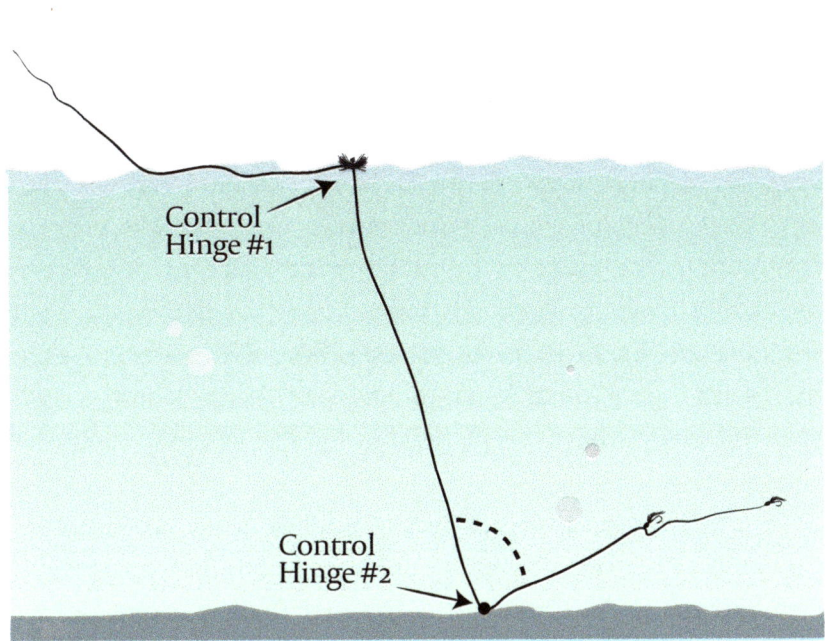

The second, obscurer hinge is created from the weight to the last fly in this rig. It also is much more versatile than it is given credit for and needs to be exploited; however, since it's subsurface and mostly difficult to observe, you have to operate on theory. Once you learn to "set" this depth, your nymphing skills will change drastically for the better. The theory is simple: the farther your flies are from the weight, the higher they will float off the bottom. This is another reason I like to run unweighted flies: I have more control over the use of this rule. If I were to rig a big weighted fly as my initial dropper in my nymph rig, this would act as the weight and negate my ability to dial in the rest of my flies in the drift. In other words, the weighted bug becomes my hinge point, thus shortening the entire rig from the split shot to the point fly.

Now, when you rig unweighted flies in a two–hinge nymph rig, two things will become quickly evident. One, the numbers of fish eating your flies will increase markedly. Two, your sets will have to be as fast as a hiccup. Without extra weight on the flies, fish don't seem to hook themselves as readily as with unweighted flies, and they can spit out flies that weigh next to nothing imperceptibly. The fish will have to move the weight before an "eat" will register; therefore, I like to fish with sensitive yarn indicators as often as possible and keep the distances between the indicator and the weight as short as possible. Keeping the distance between weight and indicator at minimum lengths quickens reaction times to fish eats. Usually I err on the side of fishing with too much indicator–to–flies distance and work my way back to shorter distances from there. As for the fish that eat and spit without detection, strive to fish the vicinity around your indicator, always on the lookout for any fish movement that you can quickly set on.

I'm lucky: I get to legally fish three flies in my home state of Colorado. Other states have different regulations on the number of flies you can use. The three–fly in–line nymph rig is as versatile as it is effective. We will dig into the versatility later, but the effectiveness of this rig is impressive when it comes to fishing a run from the bottom up. With the addition of the third fly, which is furthest from the weight hinge, I can get into the upper part of the lower water column from the bottom up. To get higher into the column with a two-fly in-line rig, simply increase the distance from the weight to the first fly in the rig. Water columns are basically theoretical divisions from the water surface to the bottom grade. The easiest way to break the water into columns is to divide the depth by three. For most of the obvious applications, that is as accurate as you need to be when vertically dividing the water. But wait, there's more! There's always more.

THE GRIDS

In my mind, simply breaking the vertical run into thirds is a bit archaic. Sure, for most recognizable applications it will work, but why not exploit the obscure and take it another couple of steps? Why not break down the vertical dimension of a run with a grid, as you would the horizontal dimension? To explain this, let's first take a look at the horizontal grid. It's observable, and the ten–percenters already have a game plan in place when it comes to applying their grid to new or old water. Experience and patience will be a large portion of how they will attack a run. The general rule they will follow will be to work the run from downstream to upstream, from near to far, systematically.

I go so far as to apply a horizontal grid to the water's surface, and painstakingly work each grid line from the bottom of the run to the top of the run and from near bank to far bank. I imagine both X and Y coordinates on the water's surface. Each point where X and Y meet is a spot I want to hit as closely as possible when I cast. The X is the axis distance away from the angler to the seam he or she wants to fish, the Y is a horizontal axis line that runs in the river seam. This line always follows the seam perfectly: if the seam flows away from the angler, the line moves with it, and, consequently, so should the drift. The point where X and Y meet is the beginning of your drift, while coordinate Y becomes a line following the seam you intend to fish during the drift.

Line Y is an axis line that must follow the movement of the seam, and the angler must stay perfectly in that line to present flies properly to waiting fish. As my clients are fishing, I often tell them to try to calmly work grid after grid, X and Y after X and Y. Once they've maxed out their casting and mending abilities or finished that portion of the run grid, they move quietly to the next section of the coverage grid.

The X axis is the distance away from the angler, the Y axis follows the seam and is rarely in a straight line. Neil Corvino pictured fishing near the headwaters of the Arkansas River, Colorado.

The faster the water's surface, the closer the gridlines and the closer each drift will be as you cover the water. I have observed many fish in faster water feed over the years. They all seem to have one thing in common when it comes to feeding in faster water: they will sway only short distances to their right or left. If they move too far to one side or the other, the current will suck them out of their hold and flush them downstream. Fish work hard to find and hold onto holding water in faster currents. The minute a fish gets flushed from its hold, boom, the next fish takes its place. Finding and keeping a good feeding line is a very competitive business for fish, and they will fight to get it and keep it. The faster water alongside the holding spot is also desirable for feeding fish, for reasons we discussed earlier. So not only is this hold a prime lie, but your drifts have to be on the money, along tight gridlines, with the indicator and flies in the exact same seam, because these fish are there to feed and your chances of hooking up are high if you pay attention to details.

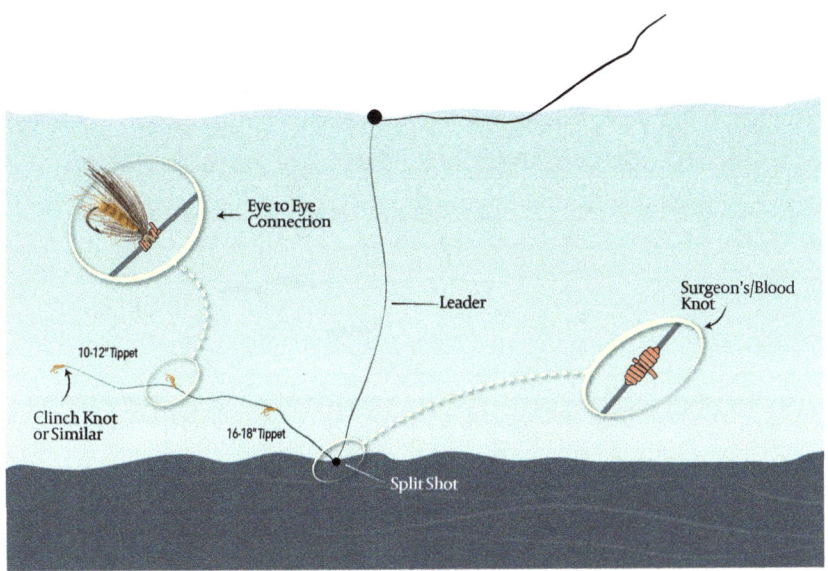

Take a look at the nymph rig diagram and notice how closely the three flies are connected. The total distance from the first to the last is around twenty inches. I do this for a reason: I want to try to have a fish see at least two of the flies as I work each grid line. If my flies are too far apart and I hit a grid line perfectly, there's a chance the fish will only see one of my offerings. Shorten those distances and watch what happens. Now you hit a grid line in faster water and a feeding fish is apt to see at least two of your flies in a zone. If the fish eats, it won't get flushed downstream by the current, but by your hook set. If I am in a "two–fly state," where regulations call for only two flies being used, then the distance between my flies will not be more than sixteen inches. In all nymph rigs, if my flies get closer than eight inches, I'll cut and apply new tippet at the correct lengths.

In all applications, the distance from the weight to the first fly is no less than fourteen inches. I like to begin each day with the weight–to–first–fly distance set to sixteen to eighteen inches. These are not numbers I just pulled from a hat, but numbers I have decided upon based on years of statistical study. I'm going with data that has been followed closely for many years on the water.

As a rule, I have found that the slower the water's surface is, the wider the gridlines can and should be placed. In slower water, as a rule, feeding fish will be more comfortable moving side to side to eat your offering. This does not mean that I will increase the distance between my flies; it only means I can apply a grid that isn't so tight or precise. Apply this thought to where you hook most of your feeding fish, the walking speed seam water next to faster or deeper water, and you don't need precise casting to move fish here. All you need in this instance is to work it down to up and near to far, with precise mends and proper depth and speeds. Cover it inside out with patience and skill, and you should do just fine.

I contend that mastering the vertical grid is more important than the horizontal grid. For sure, the two grids must be covered as one, but the fish live and feed in the vertical columns. Even fish feeding on the surface are still predominately under water, they just happen to be in the upper third of the upper column. The horizontal grid is simply a way to attack the vertical grid systematically. My bread is buttered mastering the vertical grid. If I can quickly discern where fish are feeding vertically, I have a much better chance of having a successful day.

This brings back a point I made earlier: if feeding fish are eating size sixteen (PMD) nymphs predominately, and I run a size twenty (BWO) fly at the proper vertical depth and speed, I am confident I can still catch fish. Conversely, if I am running the perfect size sixteen PMD fly, but in the wrong vertical position, it could make for a long day. This is consistent with the fly fishing formula, and I have seen it verified countless times. The formula, referring to what the angler must do to put the flies and the fish on a collision course, is so important in my fly fishing world it makes up the next chapter. Until we cover it in more detail, stay tuned and keep thinking, "Put your best bugs in the best spots with the best drifts."

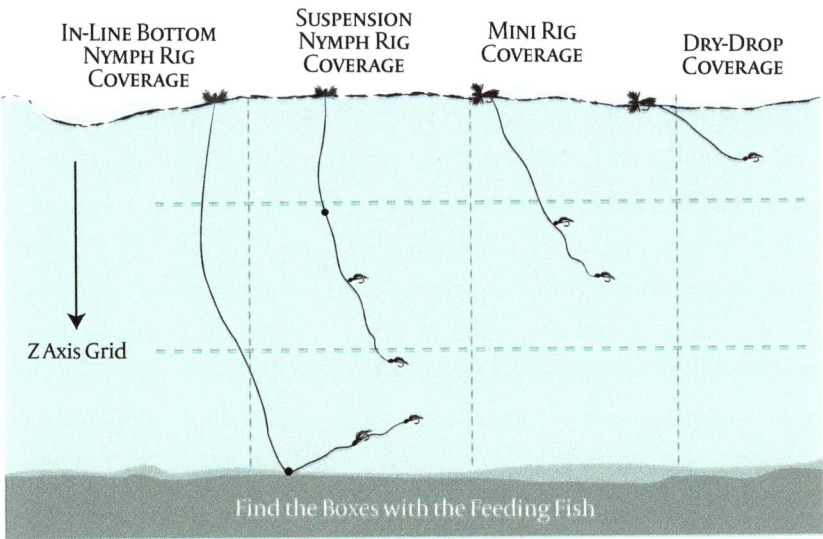

Just like the horizontal grid, the vertical grid has rules regarding how large you make your gridlines. The faster the water, the closer the grid or the smaller the boxes. The diagram of the vertical gridlines depicts a cross–section of the river as it flows toward you. It's like stepping into the river, facing upstream and placing a large section of glass perpendicular to the river flow. This gives you a great view of the columns from a protected vantage point. You'll notice both horizontal and vertical lines. The horizontal lines represent the various columns' levels; the vertical lines show divisions within the columns. The vertical lines become your Z–axis lines and the "boxes" that are formed show likely feeding fish areas depending on conditions.

I find it interesting that folks don't often think about the vertical Z–axis grids. Most are so busy trying to read the surface of the water that they forget the Z–axis or depth component. X and Y are important, but Z is critical. Fish live in the Z–axis: it's their dimension, and it's much more important than the surface of the water. Let's look back at the X and Y points within the drift. You hit your X and Y point with your cast and use your skills to keep the drift on the Y–line, while you're keeping your flies at the proper speeds and depths in the Z–axis grids. How deep is the Z–axis? As deep as the feeding fish. It's usually observable. Even if you can't see the feeding fish, you will eventually "observe" them as you work the water and begin to move a few.

Much like horizontal grids, vertical grids can become very close to one another. It's not always about the speed of the water. Sometimes an angler has to divide the vertical columns from the usual three to many more times that. This is fairly obscure, and not many people discuss or explain this, but Mama Nature has the final say when it comes to determining vertical grids. Sometimes, when fish are feeding selectively on one stage of one bug, or water temperatures drive fish into certain favorable conditions, or any combination of environmental factors converge, the angler will divide the gridlines to form boxes that are maybe the size of shoeboxes. Some days, again because of environmental factors, the fish are eating opportunistically and those same boxes may be the size of a fifty–inch television. Your job, even though most often you can't see the fish when fishing, is to find those feeding boxes through experience, knowledge, and/or experimentation. Once you find those boxes, you need to fish them properly.

As you continue through this book, you will gain knowledge on locating the boxes using experience, knowledge, or experimentation, or a combination of all three. As you continue to fly fish with the vertical boxes in mind, the entire sub–surface will begin to light up. With a little guidance and water time, you'll begin to formulate why the fish are holding in various boxes, and when it's time to throw nymphs, dries, dry–droppers, or streamers. The combination of the X–Y–Z grids and the use of the fly fishing formula (which you'll see soon), will make a difference in how you approach a river, and your fishing success But first, more foundational information . . .

Modify the Grid

There are three conditional situations you always have to contend with whenever you lace the wading boots up: water conditions that prevent you from seeing fish or content in the river, water conditions that allow you to see the river content but not the fish, and finally, water conditions that allow you to see water content and fish. The last condition is what most folks hope for, because it allows you to go right at the fish with the fly fishing formula, allows you instant feedback on fish takes, and allows you to fish "around" or modify your grid according to obstructions you can clearly see.

If you see a fish swaying side to side between two rocks in three feet of water, while it lazily eats midge larva, then with practice, you should usually be able to hook that fish. You have spied the fish from downstream, it has no idea you're there, from conditional data you've determined the fish is eating midge larva, and you can see the obstructions surrounding the fish. Your ability to set up your rig, set up your positioning, and set up and present proper casting angles is going to determine if you can get this fish to eat. You know the fly fishing formula as you rig up the correct amount of weight and indicator–to–fly depth and you allow for proper sink rates of your flies according to water speeds and fish depths. You know how far upstream to cast to allow for the sink to take place and make your flies and the fish to collide. If you don't know these things, you need more water time or a good friend or guide to work with you. This situation is a really good measuring stick of your ability.

The above scenario is simply called sight fishing. There are many times you can sight fish. You can sight nymph with a nymph rig, mini–rig (page 43), dry fly, or dry–drop sighted fish feeding on top, or swing streamers or wet flies to fish holding in any column. In other words, sighted fish give you great opportunities to test your skills. Most often, I find that when I see a fish with a client, we will determine how it's feeding (if it is), what it may be feeding on, and the best possible rig and position to work from according to my client's abilities. Most of the time we see fish feeding on the surface or feeding on nymphs subsurface, so it comes down to dry flies and nymph rigs as the weapons of choice. Whichever method you choose, there are certain rules of thumb to follow.

When you can see the fish, the fish can see you. Although that's not always true, I approach every sight fishing opportunity this way. This helps me greatly reduce my profile, use surrounding habitat as cover, minimize my movements, and slow down my approach.

If I can couple the above rules with one more important one, my chances of a hook–up escalate. Only show the fish your flies. Don't show them fly line, fly slap, or fly rod flash. Not only do you have to fish like a ninja, but you have to set up and present perfectly. Sight nymphing is the best way to hone your skills and work by the above rules, and that's why many of my anglers catch the majority of fish sight nymphing. It's just easier.

In a typical sight nymphing situation, we are working with water on the shallow side, anywhere from six to thirty–six inches is desired. This allows for a few things. First, it helps with the fly fishing formula, because we don't have to cast too far upstream, increase the distance between indicator and weight to more than five feet, or pile on the weight to get those bugs down quickly. Again, hopefully, you've had an opportunity to factor in a few things on the river, and these notions aren't foreign to you. If they are, you may want to put the book down now and go fishing! Second, with water between those two levels, it's easier to get closer using the "hip and two steps" method, and you can clearly see how the fish reacts to your drift.

The deeper and calmer the water that a fish is holding in, the easier it is for them to see you. Shallow water with a "chop," or surface that is textured by current, is your friend while sight fishing. Usually in the conditions outlined, you can line the fish's tail up with your upstream hip and take two large steps downstream to become difficult to see. If you're taller than five feet ten inches, you'll want to take three steps. These are only rules of thumb: err on the side of further away, but be careful not to outkick your coverage by gaining too much space and making it difficult to cast, mend, drift and set. Finding your "safety zone" according to your height/water depth is a matter of putting in the time on different runs, depths, and water surface conditions.

For sight nymphing, which is usually a close game, strip out the intended amount of line you wish to cast, and let it water–load downstream as you slowly lift your rod tip to roll cast position. Cast upstream as far as the formula tells you. Keep a nice, flat fly rod as you hold it as high as you need, depending on the amount of line on the water. Try not to mend, but if you have to, mend before you get near the fish. And finally, shift your fly rod tip out ahead of your indicator without applying drag to the drift. With your rod slightly in front of your indicator, you can see the fish and indicator better throughout the drift, allowing a quicker response to movement from either.

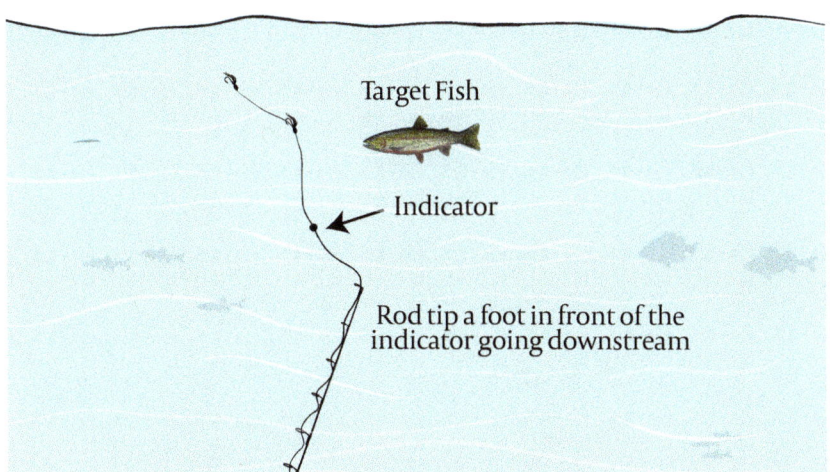

Don't let the fish see the indicator when sight nymphing and be careful not to "pull" the indicator downstream.

Sometimes on our tailwaters out west, you run into ultra–nervous fish that call for special obscure tactics to sight nymph them with regular success. Indicators in these waters can really spook the fish. Sometimes these fish blow out of holds at the mere sight of an indicator. But most often, they will stay in their hold and tolerate your indicator, but will go completely selective or altogether vegetarian. You can try to run clear and small indicators or yarn indicators to combat this, but the only two methods that I have found that really win over these trained fish is running a mini–rig or losing the bobber entirely.

The mini–rig doesn't spook these wary fish, because they are used to seeing big, dry flies on the surface. Running a sighter leader lends itself perfectly to removing the bobber and using the sighter to detect strikes. The sighter leader, which we will discuss fully later on, is a leader comprised of differently colored sections to assist in sighting drift intricacies or fish takes. You can also add a backing bead, or barrel, to the sighter for added strike detection. My backing bead is made of chartreuse or orange backing and placed in the upper monofilament section of the leader. You'd be amazed how easy it is to see and how fishing with either of these two methods will increase your hook–up rates. If you are beginning to sight nymph, I suggest you stay with a subtle indicator and work on your ability to get close and keep the indicator hidden from the target fish. This is great experience and will soon teach you the nuances of sight nymphing without an indicator if you desire.

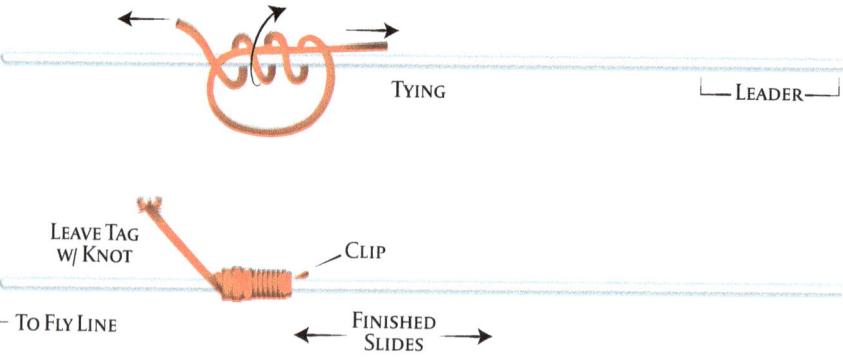

If you set up properly, cast without spooking, and drift drag-free, you don't need the perfect flies on board to catch feeding fish while sight nymphing or dry dropping. The key word in that last sentence is *feeding* fish. If you put an imperfect bug choice perfectly onto a feeding fish, there's a better than good chance it will eat your offering. If you put the perfect fly perfectly, well, you should have that fish eat every time.

When you're sight nymphing with a three-bug rig, line the middle fly in the rig with the fish's nose. This way, if you're rigged properly and in the proper vertical column, the fish should see all three of your flies. If you're running a two-bug nymph rig, line up the center of the tippet between the two bugs, and when you're mini-rigging, strive to line your bottom fly, or point fly, up with the fish at its level. Stay at or slightly above the fish's level with your lowest fly. Next, anticipate the set, trust the fish is going to eat, and be ready.

How do you know when to set when running the sight nymphing or mini-rigs? Many times, a fish will eat and spit before the indicator moves and you can set. We've gone over that dynamic already. However, when you are very close to the fish, you have an advantage if you're willing to think obscurely. Fish are like me. If I want a beer from the fridge, I go straight to the fridge, grab what I want, and then go straight back to the couch to watch the ballgame on television. Whether side to side or up and down, fish are only going to move as far as they need to eat the bug, then go right back to the holding position. Watch them as they move toward your flies, and set when they stop and begin to swing back to their original position. In many cases, you can't be certain where your flies are, but with practice and experience you can imagine where they are. Seriously, you throw the same rig consistently in various water conditions and fish holds, and you will be able to closely predict where your flies are at most any position within the drift. Keep the fish in your main window of vision, and your indicator or sighter in your peripheral or secondary window. In this way, you can keep tabs on your indicator, indicator fly, sighter, and the fish. This makes you a very potent sight fisher, no doubt.

This brings us all the way back to modifying your grid. If you can see the fish and the contents around the fish, then there is no need for a grid: you go right at the fish with X, Y, and Z coordinates and the fly fishing formula. Put the flies in the proper seam at the X and Y coordinates, allow for the flies to get to proper depth of the Z–axis, and keep the flies in the Y–axis throughout the drift right to the fish. Getting the initial cast close to perfect is important; if you put the cast in exactly the same seam the fish is in, then the rest of the equation is to ensure the drift is exactly as the naturals are drifting. Again, you must allow for the unimpeded drift around obstructions within the Y–axis with little peripheral movement of the fly rod. Casting is only a portion of this equation, and we will discuss mending techniques that can get you into the seam should you miss your mark. Folks put a huge premium on the ability to cast well, but how critical is it?

Casting is important, but if you can't provide a lifelike drift in a continuous seam in and around obstructions, it doesn't matter how well you cast. If you think about it, we just explained sight fishing with dry flies as well. All the same rules apply as before; however, when sight fishing the surface, we aren't concerned with the Z–axis or depth, only the X and Y. Don't get caught in nymph drift mode when sight fishing to rising trout. All too often, I see folks that have spied surface eaters, then gotten into perfect hip and step position with a solid tandem dry fly rig, only to cast way too far upstream of their target fish. Casting far upstream from your intended target makes it nearly impossible to stay in the proper seam or attain proper speed with little drag on the flies. It forces the angler to mend several times within the drift, possibly spooking the fish. Master the three–to–five–foot drift. Learn to pick out a feeding fish, time its feeding cadence if you can, and throw a soft–landing tandem of dries as close to the fish as you can without spooking it. Don't "flock shoot" when you see several fish surface feeding in a run. The ten–percenters know to try to pick off one at a time from inside out and downstream to upstream.

Now, let's look at a few tactics for fishing water where you can see content like rocks, bars, and logs, but because of water conditions, can't spot fish. Let's pretend there's a large rock protruding out of the surface of the river. It creates nice horseshoe-shaped seams on the surface of the water as the water is forced to go around it. You can see the obstruction clearly; therefore, you automatically modify your grid to accommodate the rock. Your horizontal Y-axis is going to be forced around the rock. Go with this and allow the presentation to flow perfectly with the surface of the water as you dial in the depth and speed.

When you can't see fish, but can see enough content to fish around, modify the grid to cover every inch of the river. Using your ability to locate likely feeding fish holds, you now begin the task of working your flies around the obstructions into likely fish holds. You can't see the fish, so you must cover the water proficiently and systematically, remembering that the faster the water, the closer your gridlines. These situations usually call for nymphing and streamers, but sometimes mini-rigs or dry dropper rigs are appropriate. You will need to make a choice on how and where the fish are feeding, and usually in this situation, a down-to-up approach is better. The water in this instance is usually too off-color to support a good surface feed by the fish, but if you happen to luck into it, by all means, take any advantage of the ability to close the gap between you and the fish because of poor visibility. Use every nymphing and mini-rigging rule to put you right on the fish. As for streamers, use a tandem set and make one of the streamers highly visible to you, so you can work around the obstructions effectively. We'll talk streamers more in a bit.

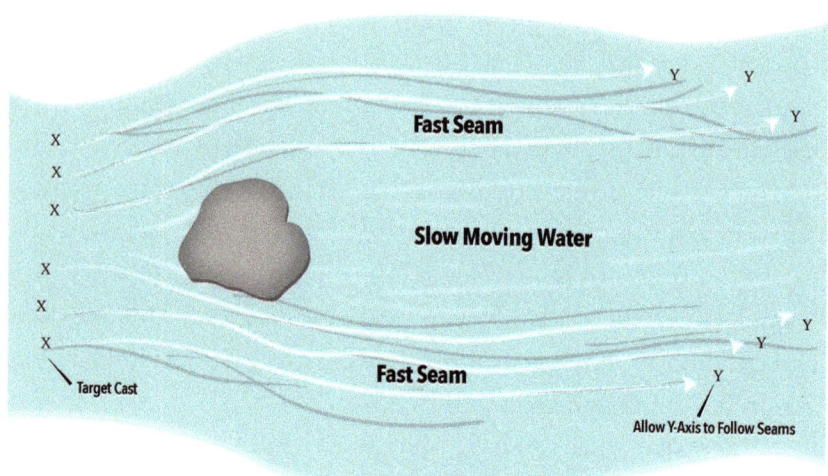

Modify Your Grid To Match Conditions

All right. We have talked about a few strategies when we can see the fish and river content, and we have discussed what you can do when you can see the content but not the fish. Now let's discuss what to do when you can't see fish or content. In most cases, in these water conditions, we are relegated to nymphing. Typically, we are talking of runoff conditions or a "blow–out" condition after a storm. Either way, we can't see fish or content. In this condition, I usually focus on two things: cover every inch of suspected holding water and work the edges like you're mad at them. The ability to "feel" your way through water like this takes ten–percenter skill, but can be gained quickly if you're willing to take a few chances. Really, the only thing you'll be risking is the flies on your rig. Since you can't see fish or content, you have to define your perimeters. Your nymph rig will easily locate the seams if you have the proper depth and speeds and you can take a few clues from the surface of the water.

You're looking for flatter or smoother water amidst the chaos, as usual, but instead of knowing where to cast and drift, you let the rig determine it for you. For example, suppose you see a flat spot in front of you, bordered on two sides by textured water. You cast into the upper portion of the smooth water, drift a couple of feet, and become hooked on some obstruction that you can't see. You probably found the upper border of the seam, or the obstruction that is causing the flat water. There's probably fish in there to catch, so free your flies and cast your flies right where you just hooked up. Hopefully, this will drop your flies right down behind this obstruction to feeding fish. I like to think I'm fishing from one "bathtub" to the next in these conditions, and I'm trying to locate the perimeter of each tub looking for fish. Each drift shows you where the obstructions are, if you are willing to get down and dirty and lose a few bugs.

The other method for hitting water that prevents you from seeing fish and content is to focus on fishing the edges. Often times, this water is flowing much higher than normal, which forces the fish to the edges for relief from the current. Just as the bottom or grade in the river slows water speeds, so do the edges. So you have two water–slowing factors right at your feet. Look for even slower water if you can find it. One such place is along the edge inside of a bend: this place is usually ripe with fish in these conditions. There are a couple of ways I will attack this situation, and both include bouncing my flies on the bottom.

First off, in this type of water situation, whether I'm fishing bathtubs or edges, my flies will be big, dark, and often weighted with a solid hot spot or contrast for added visibility. The top fly will either be a "coffee color" size ten Pat's Rubberleg or a size ten black leech pattern, followed by a purple or true fluorescent pink San Juan Worm, followed by a tungsten bead head size 16 black Soft Hackled Pheasant Tail. The leech and the soft hackle will both be tied with fluorescent pink hot spot collars.

I have had success with all levels of anglers simply drifting these rigs right along the bank; however, as the skill levels of the anglers increase, so do the options for attack. The more accomplished folks can actually get in the water, where it's safe, and perform upstream nymph drifts along the edges. This method produces great results if the fly fishing formula and drift mechanics are sound. I often encourage the advanced folks to nymph fish Czech–style, by either moving the indicator way up the leader or taking it off altogether. This technique is another modified nymphing presentation that bounces the rig weight, or weighted bugs, along the bottom without the need for an indicator. It affords the angler a chance to feel the bugs as they bounce on the bottom, and the fish when they take. There are several modifications you can make to your nymph rig to chase down this style. I've also used a "drop–shot" rig for "under the rod tip" nymphing with success. The weight goes on the very bottom of your rig, and above it about a foot away is a blood or surgeon's knot with a left–over tag to tie on your fly. I like a three–to–four–inch tag, usually in 3x or 4x tippet. You can place another tag and dropper fly above that one about another foot. Bounce that weight along the bottom or suspend it close to the bottom under an indicator, makes for some great action.

We perform the Czech knock–off technique from anywhere in the river, directly below the fly rod tip. Hold your fly rod flat to the water as you strive to "find" the bottom with your rig. Once you can feel the bugs consistently bounce on the bottom, note the distance your rod tip is above the water and remember that distance. If you're running a sighter leader, notice the portion that is in the water and use that as a benchmark. Or, once you start moving fish at one depth, tie on a backing bead, and place it on your leader to maintain that specific depth. Slide it up and down your leader to help keep you at fish–feeding depths. This drift is usually up to ninety degrees upstream to ninety degrees downstream, so line management is critical, as your flies drift toward you, then away from you downstream. The fly rod often must raise and lower a bit as the angler strips in or releases the management loop line. If you're weighted properly, you should be on the bottom, bouncing from the one–quarter mark in the drift. Again, note the rod tip–to–water distance when you begin ticking on bottom and work to keep your flies there. Be mindful not to drag the flies downstream, but to lead them as you feel them tick off the bottom. A nice slow lift of the bugs at the end of the drift produces many fine fish.

Top–Down or Bottom–Up?

It's often difficult to determine if you should attack a run from the top down or from the bottom up. Historical, seasonal, and conditional data go a long way in determining this decision. Because I take and keep extensive notes, I can most often predict how I will approach a run, and where the vertical feeding boxes may be. As a rule of thumb, I nymph bottom–up in the winter, because feeding fish are typically in deeper holds, swaying on nymphs. I'll keep working bottom–up until runoff in late May, but I will be carrying another rod or two rigged with dry flies or a tandem streamer outfit. The pre–runoff period, which is March through May in my neck of the woods in Colorado, can make for some prolific fly fishing. As fish go from swaying eight to ten inches to either side to feed in early March, to swinging, chasing, and elevating as they feed in mid–May, one needs to be prepared for approaching them bottom–up predominately, with an eye on a top–down approach. Simply put, as the water begins to rise, the water warms, and several species of bugs begin to hatch, your tactics should change with it.

I define swinging feeding fish as those that will move their body length to either side to feed. Elevating fish are not always feeding in the surface film or off the water surface. On the Eagle River, I often observe elevating fish in the middle of the middle column. They will often lift to feed an entire body length, eat, and then freight–train right back into position. It's obvious they're feeding on emergers, but because of water conditions, angling pressure, or other factors, they prefer to eat several inches below the surface. Fish that are chasing are flat–out fun to target. During this phase, I will often tell clients to leave a misplaced cast, even though it's several feet off the intended grid, only to see a fish come screaming over to gobble up the flies. Enjoy this time, because the boxes are large and cover much of the vertical plane.

As runoff begins and water is rising and sometimes off-color, the fish move once more to any holds that provide protection from the currents. The boxes become much smaller, maybe the smallest of the year, but they can be found. Many fish are forced to the river's edge, because not only do you have drag created from the bottom, but you have significant drag provided by the river bank. You may end up with several boxes stacked one on the other, and the fish are inclined to get back to swaying, lest they be forced into current and shot downstream. If you've been fishing your quarter mile, you should have an idea where to look for concentrations of fish, such as inside bends of the river, sweepers, large obstruction seams, and island points, to name a few examples.

As runoff subsides, the fish get to spread out and begin to feed in earnest. The boxes get bigger and begin to cover the entire vertical grid as fish are feeding on nymphs and mature insects and the stages between. I still focus on nymphing, but now begin to carry a mini-rig as well. The mini-rig is a dry double-drop rig that I will cover in detail later, but it will stay in the fold from this point until winter conditions.

Around July—and this schedule may vary on your river—the water temperatures and flows begin to stabilize, the fish are now in comfortable holds, and the insect hatches are fairly consistent. The boxes are usually stacked vertically in walking speed seams, in water eighteen to forty-eight inches in depth. This is tailor-made for a fly fisher. This is when I begin to focus on fishing top-down with the mini-rig, for several reasons. I still carry a nymph rig as my second choice, and the ability to quickly apply tandem dry flies is always an option. As I approach a run, I will first fish it top-down, attempting to pick off fish holding in the middle to upper columns. Throwing the mini-rig is much less obtrusive than plopping an indicator, weight, and three flies on the water. The fish are getting a bit wary of the pressure and the "plop," and don't spook nearly as much when a big dry fly hits the surface compared to an indicator. The fish are also beginning to look up more and focus on large dries and drifting flies at or above their feeding positions. I will move as many as possible in this manner, and then, to finish off a run, I'll put a nymph rig in my client's hands, with the same basic flies attached except for the large dry fly. You'd be surprised at how many we catch with the nymph rig after moving a few with the mini–rig.

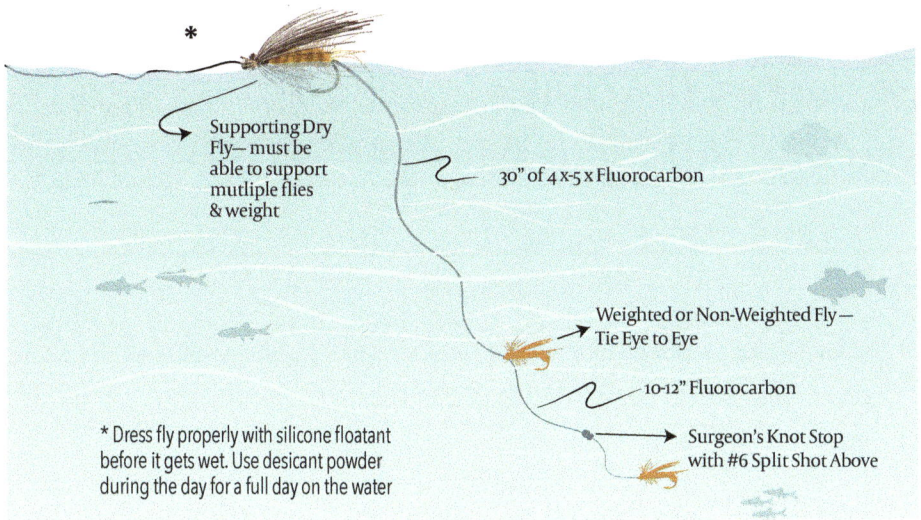

The Mini-Rig

Mini–Rig

The mini–rig is nothing more than a shallow running nymph rig with an indicator that fish will eat. There is really only one hinge point to consider, and I always make it the same depth for my droppers. With zero exceptions, the dropper is thirty inches off the back of the indicator fly, and even when you're in a two–bug state, you drop your single fly a full thirty inches below the indicator fly. When fishing the three–fly setup, it's helpful to create a knot–stop for the size six split shot with a blood or surgeons knot between your two droppers. (See diagram.) When using the single-dropper fly, do the same thing about eight inches above the dropper. Rigged this way, you can fish runs from six inches to six feet deep, in fast, slow, or still water. The only thing that changes from one type of water to the next is your casting angles and distance.

The leader you choose for the mini-rig is determined by the usual factors: size of targeted fish, water flows and clarity, fly size, size of the water fished, and personal casting preferences. This said, I like to throw the mini-rig with a seven-and-a-half-foot 4X tapered monofilament leader, with an additional sixteen inches of 4X or 5X monofilament tippet connected with a surgeon's knot. I find this fishes well in technical tailwaters and bigger freestones alike. It turns the mini-rig over well for most folks. Here's a quick hint about the mini-rig drift: try to get your indicator dry fly floating with its head pointing at you or downstream. I've noticed over the years that drifting the mini-rig with the big dry fly indicator facing upstream doesn't get as many eats on the surface or subsurface. This obscure technique can be achieved simply by using mending to turn the fly to the proper drift angle.

The bugs you select for subsurface are your call, depending on how the fish are feeding and what insects are prevalent. The large indicator fly is your choice as well, but I have a few that I rely on. I like a size eight or ten Chubby Chernobyl or Fuzzy Wuzzy to do the majority of the heavy lifting (no pun intended) for the mini-rig. Your choices may vary according to geography. Just make certain you select a fly that when dressed properly will float all day, is very visible for detecting strikes, and brings up a few fish to eat it now and then. I like to use silicone floatant, brushing it in where needed at first, and as the day wears on, a desiccant powder to keep the old girl floating. Selecting your indicator fly is as important as selecting the type of indicator you use on your nymph rig. Always keep in mind that the easier it is for the fish to see you, whether because of clear water or close quarters, the more subtle and peaceful your offerings need to be. The mini–rig indicator bug and the now–popular yarn indicators for nymphing can be less spooky to fish and more sensitive to takes. Again, water conditions and other environmental factors dictate how you proceed in choosing how to build your rigs.

The top–down approach will serve you all the way through the end of October before you switch back to a bottom–up approach for winter conditions. The dimensions of the rig remain consistent, although the flies begin to get smaller. Some years, in extended fall weather conditions, the top–down approach is still the method of choice well into November. Keep track of water temperatures, flows, and fish behaviors as you progress through the year and you will find the following year fairly predictable regarding what rig to fish when. You have to take what Mama Nature throws at you; use the best method, be it top–down or bottom–up; and keep an open mind and be willing to switch out as conditions call.

Locating the Boxes

If you're able to see the fish and how they're feeding, your chances of completing the fly fishing formula are strong as you create a collision between feeding fish and flies. If you can't see the fish and are basically "blind fishing," the systematic approach to locating feeding fish becomes critical. Look to properly fish a seam and a box at a time, and move through the sequence from either top down or bottom up. Once you've mastered the systematic approach, your ability to read both horizontal and vertical grids will be simplified and automatic. It becomes an if–then, cause–effect approach that takes the guesswork out of the drift.

George Schmidt with a dandy brown trout fooled on the
Butt Crack Baetis as the point fly in the mini rig. Eagle River, Colorado.

Provided you are rigged correctly, have read the water correctly, and have the proper depth and speed rigged, you can pick apart a run vertically and systematically. Experience and historical and seasonal data will play large parts in deciding whether you choose the top–down or bottom–up approach, as will conditional environmental factors. Historical data is data that has been collected on a long–term basis and depicts what usually happens historically; seasonal data is also long–term data, but attempts to hone into the possible outcomes in a time frame; whereas conditional data is what is going on real–time. In other words, in Colorado, we historically have a week during winter that doesn't get above freezing. That's historical data. However, seasonally, we are not sure when it's going to happen, but odds are it will occur sometime in January. We won't know conditional data we leave the house tomorrow.

One must always be on the lookout for clues to what the fish and insects are up to. If I am completely stumped and see little or no bug or feeding–fish clues, then I will default to a well–rigged nymph setup, covering various sizes and stages of insects, to locate the feeding boxes. Approaching the run in this manner, I will fish it from the bottom up, with my best drifts and confidence flies.

Confidence flies could be flies you have used before with success on similar water or just what the guy at the fly shop said the fish are eating. Either way, they go a long way in allowing you to concentrate on your drifts other than what's left in your fly box. Stack one good drift on another, work the run from the tailout to the shelf from inside out, and observe everything. Again, make sure you're at the proper depth and speed, and if you move a fish, miss a set, or hook up, file that into your brain and try to duplicate that drift on every section of the run. If you hook up solidly, try to identify what fly the fish ate before attempting to land it. When I'm fishing with friends or guiding a multi-person trip, when someone hooks up, the first question is always "What did it eat?"

Louis Grizzard said, "You fish the wrong fly long enough, and it becomes the right fly." If you're not hooking any fish, and are confident in your rigging and your flies, adjust your weight and depth again. Give the flies you've picked a chance. Clients often ask me why I don't change flies very often. First off, I'm confident of my historical, seasonal, and conditional data, and my choice on how to approach a run. Second, I'm going to change depth and speed and tactics (upstream work, angles distance, etc.) several times before I give up on the flies I've chosen. Only after I feel I've exhausted every option with the rig will I change a fly. I'll get into this more in the chapter on fly selection, but the rigs I run are set up to cover many fish food options in every drift. Give yours a chance to perform.

If I hook a fish in two feet of water moving at slightly less than walking speed, then I will seek out that specific water and work it like I'm mad at it. That's a simple cause-effect relationship, but you have to be hooking fish to put it in play. If you begin to hook fish in the upper pool section of a run, after you've pinched on some weight putty to slow down your drift, then you seek out similar runs and parts of the run. Let's say you've been hooking fish in the upper pool for a while and the bite stops. You can either move to the next section or begin to fish the same run in the next column up. Here, you can reduce indicator–to–weight depth or increase that depth and reduce weight while changing casting angles to more upstream. Starting to get the idea?

If I want to fish higher in a column in the same run I've been fishing, depending on water depth, I prefer adding indicator–to–weight distance while reducing weight over reducing indicator–to–weight distance. In other words, I opt for more distance over increased rig weight. If the run is substantially deep, say six feet or so, I have no problem reducing the indicator–to–weight depth, because in this instance you're usually not going to spook fish with the indicator. If I am in shallower water, where to get into that middle column I will have to move the indicator to within four feet of my weight, I will opt for added length and less weight. I may go from a BB–sized split down to a number–four split and increase my indicator to weight depth another foot, while adjusting casting angles. I call this my long and lean nymph rig, because of the additional indicator–to–weight length and the reduction in weight. This allows me to fish the run in the middle column effectively, provided I account for casting angles and distances.

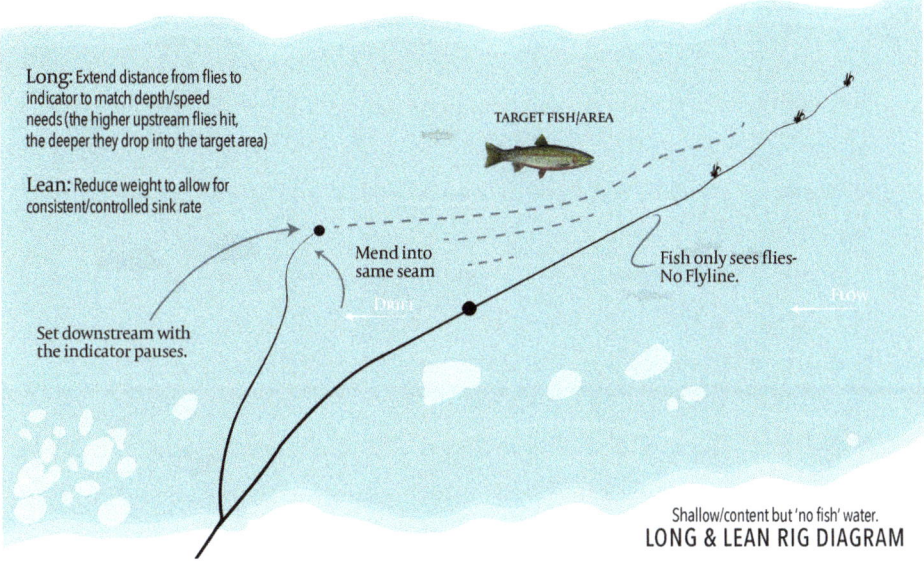

LONG & LEAN RIG DIAGRAM

To make this obscure technique work, you must concentrate your efforts on the upper half of the drift. If you present correctly here, it will put those flies right where you want them in the middle column. Your indicator will then be downstream of your target area, well out of the fish's view, and your unweighted flies will drift lifelike right down the zone. Long and lean nymphing also performs well in shallow water down to six inches in the depth. In the following chapters, we will continue to dig into this rig and even more obscure drift methods and rigs.

Not always do you need to bounce the weight in an in–line nymph rig on the bottom. Sometimes you can't do this effectively at all. Sometimes water conditions and fish feeding behaviors call for suspension rigs under an indicator. Think of them as dry–dropper rigs or mini–rigs, only at vastly deeper depths, as you search for the "feeding boxes." I have never liked to run an indicator within forty inches of my first dropper in my nymph rig. That's what the mini–rig is for, because even with a subtle, unobtrusive, small yarn indicator, I could be spooking fish. However, suspended rigs do have a place in my nymphing arsenal occasionally.

I find suspended rigs very useful in deeper pool sections that have suspended feeding fish. The idea is to identify which vertical box along with Z–axis depth is producing the most feeding fish, and align your depth accordingly. If you've done any suspended nymphing in still water, you know what I'm talking about; the indicator simply supports the entire rig without the flies or weight touching the bottom. If I can see the feeding fish, I will estimate the depth from the indicator to my bottom fly to the fish's nose. I want my flies at or above the fish's level. If I am "blind nymphing" a deep pool run and can't observe feeding fish, I will start by fishing as close to the bottom as possible and working my way up the column in search of feeding fish. Once you begin finding feeding fish at a certain depth, you can really dial in your presentations.

There are certainly more qualified anglers than I out there, who have specialized skills in nymphing deep runs with suspender rigs. Once I get to the point that I'm sinking twelve feet of leader under an indicator, or when I need to employ slip bobbers, I will go to the next spot. There are just some situations and techniques I'd rather not employ on moving water, and super–deep, suspended nymphing is one of them.

So far, we've systematically worked from the bottom up. Now it's time to look at attacking a run from the top down. There comes a time when you have to ditch the bottom–up approach and change methods. This is where the mini–rig shines: when you're seeing fish in the top column, you're seeing fish feeding in the film, or when data and experience dictate you fish with a dry dropper. The mini–rig provides the ability to cover the upper column, the film, and in certain circumstances, the surface. For every fish I observe feeding on emergers in the film or dries on the surface, I feel there are three more in the upper column subsurface that are feeding just as hard. Unlike having to shorten the nymph rig or going long and lean, the mini–rig affords you the advantage of getting right on top of your feeding fish without worrying about spooking them, provided they don't see your fly line.

You can work the mini–rig close to you or as far as your casting and mending skills allow, and it's great for beginning anglers, because it helps keep the indicator fly and droppers in the same seams. Looking at the mini–rig diagram, you will notice that there is a size six split shot placed between the bottom two flies. If you remove that weight and apply floatant to the tippet, you can get your droppers perfectly in the film for a wonderful drag–free drift. One of the few times I will tie and use flies with weighted beads is when the fish are feeding below the surface in the upper column. If the weighted bead does not supply the rig with a quick enough sink rate for presented conditions, like faster water, then place the number–six split shot in the usual place between the two droppers.

The beauty of the mini–rig, other than allowing you to effectively fish many different types of water, is that not only does the top indicator fly show you when there's been a take, but it's not unusual for fish to come up and yawn in that big dry. This happens most often when large adult stones or hoppers are present, but I've hooked fish on the big dry every month of the year in Colorado. The mini–rig dimensions are set. If you target fish in a certain grid horizontally and vertically that requires a different depth presentation, adjust the angle and distance of your cast to satisfy the formula.

Finding a good hatch and fish feeding in earnest on the surface is always fun. When I get into this situation, I always take a few moments to observe. Sometimes this drives my clients crazy, but I do it for a couple of reasons. First, I want my clients to settle into the river and the cadence of fish feeding on the surface. This is as critical as the flies you choose, because you need to relax and devise a game plan. Second, we want to be able to carefully set up in the best position to begin a surgical approach, an approach which offers us the best chance to hook more than one fish. We will determine where we are best hidden from view, how we will approach the run, and what types of casts we are qualified to pull off. Again, it's a systematic, cause and effect process that determines our approach. Last, in nearly every dry fly fishing opportunity I get, I will throw tandem dry flies dimensioned exactly the way I want them. Alas, this is for a later chapter. Until then, let's dig into the importance of rig dimensions.

Dimensions

I think it has become clear that each skill piggybacks onto the last. It's like learning mathematics: one skill sets you up for the next, methodically. A good foundation is key to progressing to the next step; therefore, there are a few foundational items that can't be overlooked. That brings forward the importance of the consistency of your rig's dimensions. If an angler continually switches the dimensions of a rig, he or she will take much longer when it comes time to be able to "see" the flies underwater, even though they aren't visible. I've mentioned this before, and it's worth repeating, the more consistently you rig and the more correctly you fish that rig, according to the formula, the more your brain takes over and tells you where your flies are in any water you drift. Finding the vertical boxes is hard enough; continually changing your rig's dimensions makes it even more difficult to work a run correctly.

Let's say you've been running an in–line nymph rig most of the day that you tied earlier that morning. After working the river, you've found the type of water and the feeding boxes the trout are feeding in. You're having a ball moving from one selected section to the next, until you snap off your rig on a large rock. No worries, you have all the flies and materials you need to re–tie. You re–tie the same flies, same profiles, color, and order on your fresh rig. You are back to fishing in mere minutes, but things have suddenly gone quiet. Ever had this happen to you? Bet it was your rig dimensioning. It doesn't take much to take your drift out of the proper boxes, an inch or two here or there, can and do, make a big difference in the final drift mechanics.

I am very careful to rig as consistently as possible. Take the mini–rig, for instance. I know the length of my inseam, so after tying on the top indicator bug, I can measure almost the exact dimension every time by dropping the bug down my leg to my ankle bone before snipping the tippet. My neck lanyard with all my tippets attached really helps with this method. I also know the distance between the chest clips for my shoulder straps on my waders. The inches between the two droppers are measured there. I know where to measure the distance for my nymph rig flies, and how far my wing span is when it comes to checking leader lengths. It only takes a few moments to find a way to check your measurements in your own way, but this obscure little trick is often overlooked. It most assuredly handicaps your ability to use this trick, however, if the dimensions of your rigs are inconsistent.

If you consistently are consistent, you will begin to put more trout in the net. The systematic approach gives you the chance to truly pick apart a run horizontally and vertically, as it helps you locate those feeding boxes quickly after reading the river. It takes the guesswork out of your approach and simply lets you progress to the next option automatically. As you get more familiar with this approach and the consistency it involves, you can begin to experiment and take fly fishing risks on the water. And that's when things really start to get interesting.

Fly Fishing Formula

SPEED OF THE water, rate of sink, depth of feeding fish. I remember that when I was a kid, probably ten years old or so, Dad would drop me off at the local pond on his way to work. I would have my old eight–foot Fenwick, Automatic fly reel, aluminum clip fly box, a PBJ and a canteen of water. I'd stay all day and would only leave as he picked me up on his way home. I did this most days during the summer for several years.

The majority of the fish in that old pond were bluegills with a few largemouth bass, and it was my first experience with the fly fishing formula. I didn't realize it until many years later, but those days at the pond were the foundation of what I believe today about fishing, especially fly fishing. When I fly fish, I intend for the flies to collide with fish. The only way to arrange for that collision is to calculate what it's going to take to put your offering right on or slightly above the fish's mouth. Give the fish no choices but to eat it or get out of the way.

Now that old pond was unmoving still water, and the formula calls for calculating the speed of the moving water. However, the formula still works for still water. You simply take out the speed part of the equation and focus your efforts on rate of sink and depth of feeding fish. On windy days fishing still water, speed of the water moving under the wind does come into play, but not as a general rule. Most days, you focus on getting your flies into the zone quickly (rate of sink), and putting them right on the beak of feeding fish.

Bluegills are pretty voracious little eaters. I can remember many occasions where I would sneak up on a suspended bluegill, extend my fly rod out to its full length, and gently submerge my weighted wooly worm down to the fish's level. As I had only a couple of feet of leader out, the fish usually only saw the fly. I would watch the fish intently as it studied the wooly worm. Sometimes they'd swim toward it a bit, then back off, and I'd twitch it ever so slightly to elicit a ferocious eat. Other times, the fish would notice the fly, swim toward it, only to stall out and begin to lose interest. Each time they began to swim away, I'd twitch or move the fly. Sometimes they'd be enticed to follow more or even eat it, but most often they'd lose complete interest and slink off. Sometimes, the instant I dropped the fly in front of them, they'd smash it.

The point I'm making is, even bluegills when fooled are still mostly discerning. They are still cautious, but if you continue to place a lively fly in the proper zone, more often than not you will get attention. Maybe they don't always eat it, but you often get attention.

Now, let's apply this to moving water. You still strive to provide for the fish and the fly to collide, but most often the fish has to make a much faster decision whether or not to eat your bug. This works in our favor for sure, because this creates competition between fish and our flies don't always have to be perfect.

Fly Fishing Formula

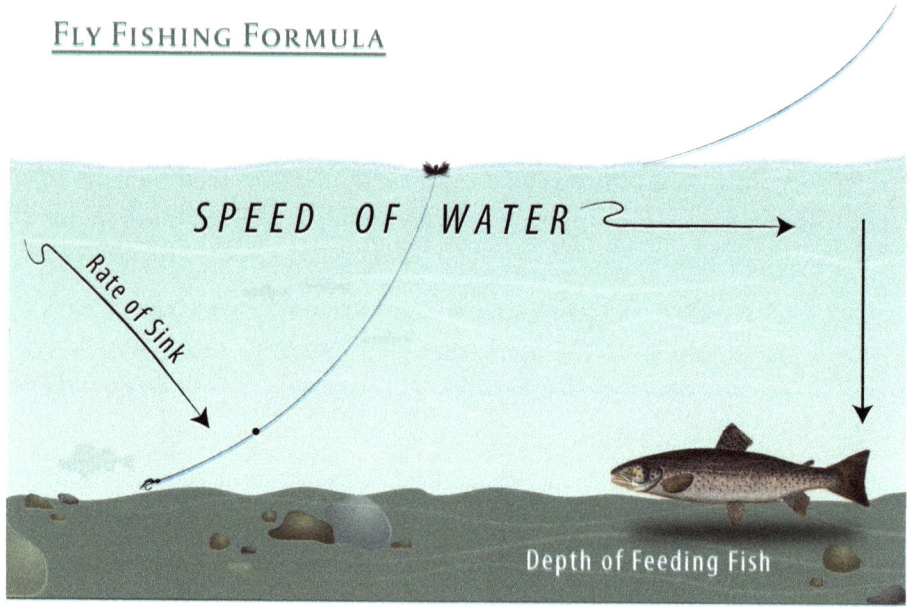

No Luck to It

If you have fished for any length of time, it's a sure bet that you've had the following scenario happen to you at least once. You've been fishing a run without much success and you've lost complete confidence in your fly rig. You decide to switch out a nymph, so you let the fifteen feet or so of line trail downstream of you while you grab for your fly box. You tuck your rod under your arm as you open your fly box to pick out the next bug. With your attention solely on the box, all a sudden you get a great jolt on the fly rod as a fish eats one of your flies suspended several feet downstream. Lucky, right? Wrong, there's no luck to it!

Just because you weren't actively fishing doesn't mean that was luck. All it means is you put the fly at the proper speed and proper rate of sink at or above a feeding fish, and it exercised the option to eat. Like with the bluegill that smashed the fly the instant it saw it, you enticed that trout in one way or another to eat your fly. The luck comes in because you didn't drop your fly box in the drink. Feeding fish eat caddis pupae regularly, as the bugs migrate to the surface to completely hatch. Sometimes those pupae get hung up in the current as they elevate or hang in the current by a silk thread. So they make an easy target for feeding fish. No luck involved. The real question here is how many of you realize the obscurity of this and begin to use techniques suited for targeting fish feeding like this.

In the previous scenario, folks that don't know tend to think that was a lucky catch, but those that understand the formula understand why that fish ate a fly suspended in the current. I wish it were always that easy, but unfortunately, it's not. Most often, in moving water, you're drifting the flies to waiting fish, not suspending the flies into the current awaiting a take, but this is simply one small example of an obscurity of fly fishing: why and how fish eat where they do. Those that are advanced anglers can almost predict why and how the fish will eat on a given day because of knowledge from experience, observing all data, and a firm handle on the fly fishing formula. Advanced anglers, your ten–percenters, have a thorough working knowledge of depth, speed, angles, and how those components work together.

Let's first delve into the nymph drift, because when people talk speed, they most often think of a subsurface drift. Speed, however, applies to all types of fishing, not just the nymph drift. Even fishing a live worm under a bobber in a still water pond requires attention to speed. From trolling lures for sailfish to drifting size twenty–two spent Trico patterns in a back eddy, speed is critical. All that said, we will begin with the foundation of the drift, the nymph drift in this case, and begin to really break down how speed works in the drift and ways to control it.

To get the proper rate of sink of your flies and the proper pace of your flies in the nymph drift current, you need to control speed. You can have the proper pace of your flies in the current at the wrong depth and still catch fish. That's how critical speed is. Speed in the nymph drift represents living insects, even though when you attain the perfect speed, folks refer to it as a dead drift. The "dead" part is referring to zero drag. If your speed control is off, your imposters won't look realistic, and fish will respond by going vegetarian. They won't eat. Simply put, speed within the drift represents the speed in that particular spot, in that particular run, of the real insects present at that particular time. There are two factions here at work: one is the ability to get your flies on a collision course with feeding fish, the other is attaining and maintaining proper pace after you get your bugs in the zone quickly.

Drift speed is mostly controlled by weight in a nymph drift. Weight adds mass to the setup, which produces drag, which slows the rate of travel. Mending the line to prevent dragging or pulling the flies unnaturally is critical if you ever really wish to progress to the next level. The better you become at mending, the less weight you need to overcome the drag supplied by the fly line pulling on your flies. In short, you will become proficient at using the absolute minimum weight to assist in slowing down your flies in the nymph drift. Let's look at it this way: you wouldn't add weight to a big grasshopper dry fly, would you? Let's imagine that you could and it wouldn't sink. What would be the effect? It would slow it down, of course. Slowed down, the big dry fly wouldn't float naturally on the surface, and would make it difficult to fool fish that are used to feeding on the real thing. If you wouldn't over–weight a bug on the surface, why would you over–weight a bug subsurface? Point is, you want the minimum amount of weight you can get away with in all types of drifts to get as close to realistic presentations as possible. The ability to mend the fly line then becomes critical.

Once you're proficient at the mend, you can begin to nymph a run with the correct speed. Some folks never quite attain this level of proficiency, but when nymphing, just like when drifting dry flies, there's really no excuse to never dial in the speed of the drift, because it is observable. You can see it, and you can see the effects of adding or subtracting weight. When you are indicator nymphing, the general rule is that you want your indicator traveling at half the speed of the water's surface. Because of the dynamics of moving water, the surface is moving about twice as fast as the water at grade. This is only a general rule, and I actually would argue that the water at grade is moving much more slowly than half the speed of the water at the surface, because of all the obstructions usually present. A good rule of thumb, however, for those just starting is to get that indicator slowed down.

The best way to observe the speed of the indicator or surface flies is to compare them to anything floating on the surface. I like to use a bubble line to compare speeds of indicator/dries to water surface, but a well-placed stick or leaf will accomplish the same. Remember: add weight to slow it down.

When you're dry fly fishing, it's preferable to get your dry fly (or flies) moving the same speed as the naturals on the water. When you're dry-dropping or mini-rigging with a dry fly and subsurface flies, it is accepted that this rig will travel slightly slower than a normal dry fly drift because of the added weight below the dry fly. This can be advantageous to less skilled fly fishers, as it helps to slow down the drift a bit and eats up some drift speed caused by incomplete mending.

Let's imagine that the speed of our nymph rig is perfect. It is going the exact speed of the naturals the fish are eating. How do you know it's the perfect speed? Your brain will be able to calculate speed for you with increased accuracy the more you fish. I've handed you the guidelines, but the game changes when your feet are wet and you're drifting bugs. That said, once you're confident the speed is sound, dial in the depth. When you're first starting out, you will learn to determine one component and then the other, but frankly, depth and speed are one. They are two distinct concepts, but one has to function with the other properly, like each wing on a flying bird. Before we dig deeper into this subject, let's define depth as the depth of feeding fish in a specific part of the run in a specific location. The location is the exact spot horizontally and vertically of a feeding fish.

The goal of nymphing is to be able to drift your flies at the proper depth and speed in the longest run as possible. Unless you're sight–nymphing and targeting one fish, you want to attain the perfect drift and maintain it until your line tightens at the end of a drift. To control depth, one simply moves the indicator closer or further away from the dropper flies. In my in–line nymph rig, the depth is controlled from the weight to the indicator, unless we are fishing it suspended in deeper water.

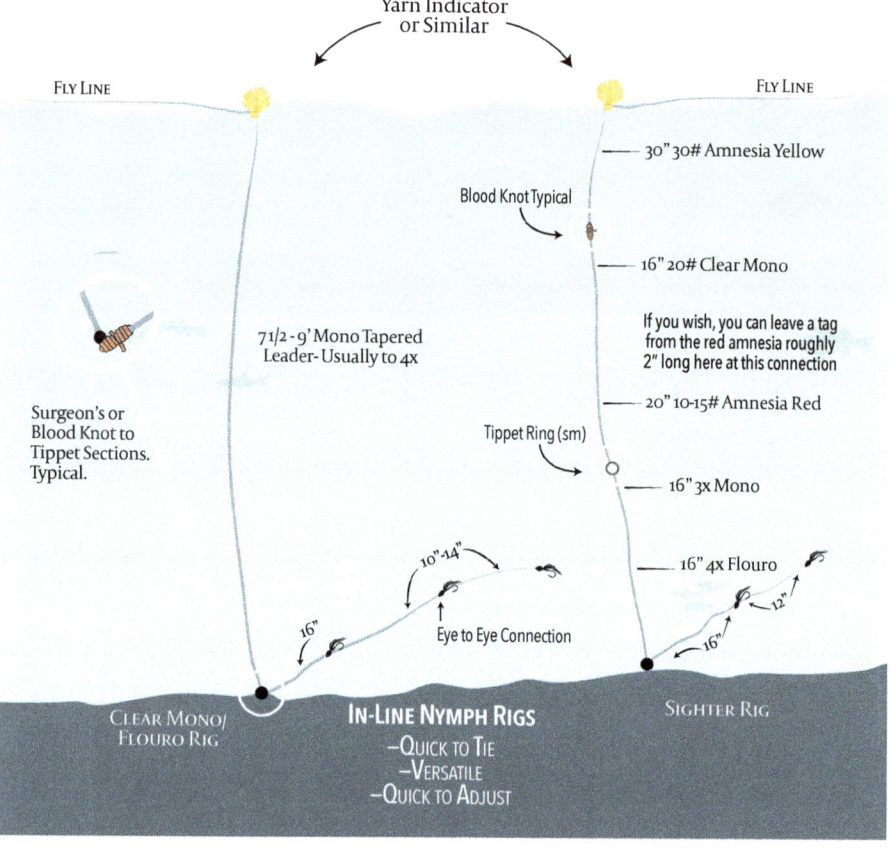

Experiment with colors, lengths and leader structures to truly customize your own sighter or tapered leader according to what the water and fish call for.

No Guesswork

How do you know when you have perfect depth? Again, this is usually observable if your weight is set to tick the bottom during the drift. If you can physically observe the rig bouncing along the bottom, you're there. But it's not always that clean and easy. Clients often ask if we should shorten our depth because we are frequently getting hung up on the bottom. But just because we are getting hung up does not mean we are running the rig too deep. On the contrary, we are probably running good depth, but need to change our drift line because we've found an obstruction big enough to foul us. Let this sink in: refrain from immediately changing the depth until you have completely read the river and searched for every drift line. I tell folks all the time: if your nymph rig is well tuned with depth and speed, you are able to feel the bottom and define the perimeters of your drifts systematically. That obstruction you keep hitting is your friend. If it's big enough to foul you, it's big enough to hold a fish or two. You need to change your drift line and work with and around the obstruction, with obscure drift and mend techniques that we will hit later on.

Here's another question I get a lot when it comes to depth and the nymph drift. Certain times of the year our rivers go through an algae bloom that, for lack of a better term, "gunks" up the river bottom. Every drift presents the opportunity to pick up the gunk off the bottom and in the water columns. When you're having to nymph because conditions call for it, it becomes a major pain when each drift collects piles of algae. The dilemma can be that the fish are feeding off the bottom, calling for nymphing, but getting a clean drift is difficult at best. This sure can be frustrating. There's a couple of things you can do in this situation: one, go long and lean with your nymph rig, decreasing weight and increasing length, or two, dry–drop or mini–rig the run. When you go long and lean, shift your thinking to working more upstream angles in this case. You're still going to pick up gunk from mid–drift down, but you can effectively fish the upper half of the nymph drift with greatly reduced "gunk–ups". Don't discount the dry–double–drop mini–rig, even in winter. I have several videos of picking up fish in the dead of winter with the mini–rig. It's obscure and unorthodox, but effective.

Where You Hooking Up?

The best way for me to describe having depth and speed work as one is to describe a scenario I see often on the river and give a few remedies that include depth, speed, length, and casting angles. Standing near my intermediate level client's hip, confident I have dialed in depth and speed as closely as I can to his mending skills, I notice where we are hooking the majority of the fish in the nymph drift. Typically, we are hooking the majority of the fish from the final one–quarter of the drift to the swing stage. We're catching fish, so I keep jabbering about mending skills, anticipating the next mend, and about proper set mechanics. Soon my client mentions something about how all the fish we are hooking are "down there" in the drift and that maybe we should move there to put them right in front of us.

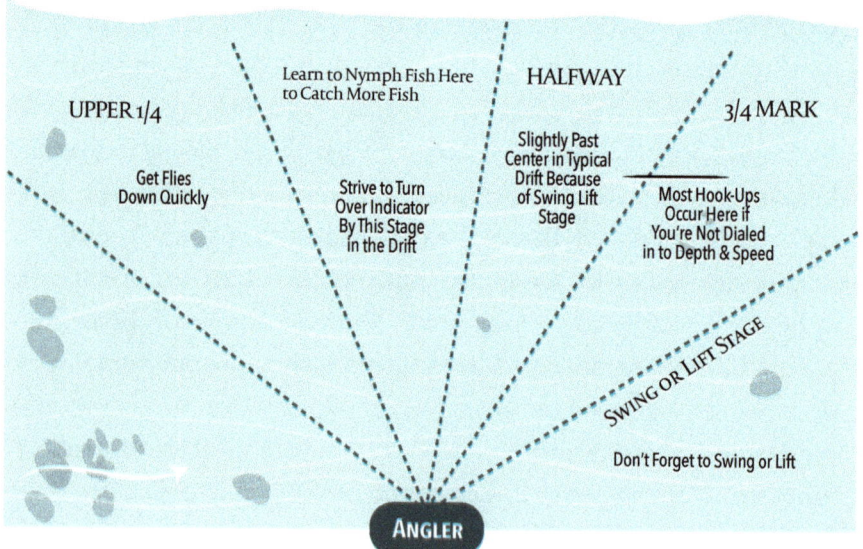

Typical Nymph Drift Stages

At this point, I have to explain what's going on. Our depth and speed are not working as one until we get to that point in the drift. Usually, I can assure the client that there are fish scattered the entire length of the drift, but we are only in perfect depth and speed at that point, which is why the fish are only eating there. With beginner to intermediate anglers, this usually occurs because their mending skills and line management are still a work in progress, but with advanced anglers, it goes beyond that and other factors are in play. It becomes a great learning experience for the beginner and intermediate–level anglers because as they improve their drift management skills, the trout begin to feed in the majority of the drift, not in just one section.

I'm often asked, "Well, what if are hooking fish upstream in the initial part of the drift, then?"

I answer with, "Life is good—enjoy it—because we're dialed in."

Now for the advanced anglers there are a few obscurities we should point out. Even though you may be certain your depth and speed are perfect, if you notice that you are hooking up constantly in the latter portions of your nymph drift, something is amiss. There is usually something going on structurally and hydraulically that is preventing you from getting depth and speed to mesh, provided you are certain you are well mended throughout the drift. I have seen this dozens of times, and it usually requires subtle changes to depth, speed, length, angles including body positioning, and mend techniques. Let's keep digging.

Imagine you are working a riffle that filters over a shelf, which flows into an upper pool section. This is flowing from your left to your right. Your cast length is about fifteen feet and you're casting up on the upper shelf at about an eleven–o'clock angle. You have the depth and speed dialed in, but continue to hook fish in the three–quarter mark of your nymph drift. You know there are feeding fish higher in the run, right on the shelf and not only where you keep hooking up. For the sake of discussion, let's say there is a huge boulder to your left that prevents you from shifting your position higher in the run. What to do?

Although it may look barren, this neat little shelf on the Dream Stream has produced many fine fish over the years when fished properly.

Your first move is to cast higher up above the shelf onto the riffle section. Strip five or so feet off your reel, cast at the same angle, and observe your drift. You should be coming off the riffle onto the shelf properly now, with your bugs now in deeper position at the proper speed. If you get hung up on the riffle section above the shelf when you cast, clear the bugs, clean them off, and cast *exactly* where your flies were just hooked up on bottom. We are trying to creep the flies over the shelf exactly like the naturals at exactly the same location, depth, and speed. If you continue to hook on the shelf, don't change your depth or speed: we know it's right. Instead, continue to cast exactly where you hooked the riffle section, and work your way incrementally down onto the shelf. As you can deduce, step one in this scenario is increasing casting length at the same angle.

If you're still not moving fish off the shelf, it's time to go to step two, which involves casting angles and additional length. Fishing is called angling for a good reason. You can control depth and speed by changing casting angles or changing casting angles and adding length to the cast. Typically, casting angles when nymphing are employed to cast at a sharper angle upstream. This allows for the flies to sink to proper depths as you drift toward your target area. At times, if it's safe, direct upstream nymph work can be deadly efficient, because you get the flies with less drag into the intended zones. This greatly reduces fly line drag, because you do not have to deal with a lot of side pressure from the current on the fly line. Think about throwing a long rope across the river compared to throwing it directly upstream. If you throw it across the river, as you retrieve it, a large downstream bow is developed. But if you throw it directly upstream, no bow will develop. All you have to do then is maintain the proper retrieval speed to keep it in a fairly straight line.

Step three: if you're still not hooking fish in the upper part of the indicator nymph drift, it will behoove you to learn to pause your indicator after the upstream cast, wait for your flies to get a good sink going, then release your indicator into the flow. When working upstream in this manner, it helps if you can pile or stack several mends on top of one another, then pick them up after your flies have had the chance to get to a fairly good depth. We will discuss these methods in more detail later, but rest assured, there are several ways to get those bugs down in the upper part of your nymph drift so you can fish it effectively.

When I begin to coach anglers on upstream casting angles, I often decrease weight and increase depth. As I remove weight, I add distance between the indicator and the bugs. This adjustment allows you to still fish effectively, getting the flies where they need to be while you are preventing constant hook–ups on the bottom. Increasing fly–to–indicator distance, if drifted properly, can make your rig behave as if you've added weight. Some may be wondering how this works, but it does. You'll just have to experiment. Even in riffles eighteen inches in depth and less, walking speed or faster, this method is very effective. In water such as this, it's not uncommon for me to run a BB–sized split shot or less, five feet from the indicator, with unweighted flies. Again, try it for yourself.

In late fall, when the water I fish is becoming skinny or at very low flows, I often find my client rigs running a full six feet between indicator and flies, with a size four split shot drowning the whole thing. You have to take what Mama Nature gives you, and this rig has been tweaked over many years. What it does is allow for a solid drift in low flows by allowing the flies to be at depth without constantly hooking the bottom. It also helps prevent the fish from seeing fly line or the indicator, which could spook them. When fishing with this long and lean rig, just mind your casting angles as outlined above, imagine target areas, and stack one good drift after another.

If you're working an abrupt shelf (shown) attempt to cast as close to the shelf as possible. When working a sloping shelf, work your way down the shelf incrementally to ensure your flies are traveling the same course as the naturals. Here, the author is a solid four feet into the drift, off the shelf, working a mini-rig.

What if, because of structure or other impediments, you can't change your casting angle? In this case, you're most often going to have to add weight to get your flies into the target zone quickly. I like to use one of the weighted putty products on the market, because I can customize the weight quickly and in small increments. Putty is much more versatile than adding another split shot or having to change to a weighted fly to help slow down your rig, because you can use what is called for instead of having to readjust angles, length, and depth after you have it dialed in. In this scenario, you have to experiment incrementally with how far you can cast upstream, and adjust your weight accordingly. You want your flies to sink as quickly as possible in a short drift, so a specialty tuck cast and a high–stick approach with a few slack mends may be in order. We will certainly talk about these skills in detail later.

There's More!

There are a few other things to look for that will give you important clues to your drift. One thing you can do is watch where in the drift your indicator "turns over." By this I mean when the leader below it straightens out and flips the indicator, to the point where the tie in spot is against the water. This is observable: you can physically watch the indicator turn over. In most drift situations, I want my indicator to turn over within the first quarter of the drift. This tells me my speed is close to perfect. You can also take a tip from the European–style fly fishers and keep an eye on your leader throughout the drift's initial stages. This will tell you how quickly you're getting proper depth and speed as you near the target area, and allows for fine–tuning. When you're rolling the mini–rig, watch for the subtle drop in floating speed of your big dry fly. You want this rig to be at perfect speed in the upper quarter of the drift as well.

I mentioned the sighter leader in the last chapter, now is a good time to dig deeper into the subject. Many of my clients like it when I place a section of sighter leader in conjunction with an indicator, and it really helps them observe the relationship between indicator and leader. Not only does this help the angler learn when the indicator turns over in drift situations, it will also help in strike detection. When a fish takes our fly in a nymphing situation, the weight must be moved to move the indicator. We already know we're dealing with two hinges, and our set time may be further impaired if we have a large amount of leader between flies and indicator. To help anglers out with subtle strike detection, I will also on occasion use a sighter about two feet above the flies, built into the leader. A ten-to-twelve-pound Amnesia section in red is my preferred sighter, but other colors work well too depending on water conditions.

If you're using a nine-foot leader (4X in this example), simply cut the leader three feet from the fly line connection, add eighteen inches of colored sighter in twenty- or thirty-pound test, and then cut out the same amount from your leader and reattach the remainder of your leader. I like to use twenty-pound Amnesia in yellow for the upper section as it really stands out and is visible. That will take care of the upper section to detect indicator turnover. For the lower section sighter above the flies, I will replace the last twenty inches of the leader with ten-to-twelve-pound red Amnesia line and then add my sixteen to eighteen inches of 4X monofilament tippet from there. On the upper blood knot between the red Amnesia and monofilament, you can leave a couple of inches of the red Amnesia tag above the knot. This short piece of line absolutely helps in tracking the sighter and detecting strikes. Surprisingly, it rarely gets hung up and knotted while fishing.

It's a good idea to use blood knots for all these junctions. You will hardly notice any effect on the leader's ability to turn over with the cast, and the benefits certainly outweigh any negative effects from adding the section into your leader. With a seven-and-a-half-foot leader (4X), do the same, but cut your leader and place in the section at two feet from the fly-line butt. Whether the indicator is above the sighter or attached within the sighter section, you can actually observe the leader sinking into the water during the drift. This can be a huge advantage for beginners to advanced anglers, because it takes out the guesswork of when your indicator is turning over. I like to put in both sighters when I'm out nymphing on my own, and soon you'll be watching the sighters as much if not more than the indicator. It's a highly simplified method that is very effective. It's obscure.

I will often construct my own sighter suspension leaders out of raw materials. For a nine-foot leader, begin with three and a half feet of Thirty-pound Gold Stren. Tie a perfection loop at the head of this to connect to your leader and use a blood knot to connect to the next thirty-inch section of twenty-pound clear monofilament. To the monofilament, connect a twenty-inch piece of fifteen-pound test red Amnesia (blood knot), then attach a tippet ring using an improved clinch knot. Now attach a sixteen-inch piece of 3X or 4X fluorocarbon tippet, and to this attach another sixteen-inch section of 4X fluorocarbon tippet. The knot (a double or triple surgeon's is recommended) in between the last two sections of 4X flouro is in case you want to use split shot on the leader. It takes pretty big water for me to run this leader rig, because the total length from perfection loop to last fly is pushing twelve feet. Use this rig when you're sure that you will need to have the indicator attached inside the upper Gold Stren section. This way, it will clearly tell you when that indicator is turning over.

A great way to learn what's going on between your indicator and flies is to employ a sighter leader.

To create an eight–foot leader (or thereabouts) with the same materials requires thirty inches of the Gold Stren, sixteen inches of the fourteen–pound clear monofilament, twenty inches of the ten/twelve–pound red Amnesia line (add tippet ring) and sixteen inches of 3X fluorocarbon tippet, then sixteen additional inches of 4X fluorocarbon added with a double surgeon's (refer to diagram on pg 74). This is my go–to sighter rig the majority of the year on waters I guide, and it can be easily customized to your liking by adding or subtracting sections as you wish.

The split–shot weight for this rig goes at the junction of the 3X and 4X tippets, and don't be surprised when this rig calls for more weight to slow it down than you're used to. The extra weight needed is fine: it won't hamper the liveliness of the rig. One note here is to keep that last section of 4X fluorocarbon a legitimate sixteen inches. Anything less than that and the red Amnesia may spook fish. Having fished this rig in all types of water and flows, including gin–clear shallow water, I can honestly say that if you keep the last two tippet sections to the specified lengths, you will be hard pressed to spook fish. Total length from the fly line junction to the last fly in a three–fly inline rig, for this particular setup, is about eleven feet. As always, experiment as you wish: customize the leader to fit your style and your quarter mile. You will find different lengths of leaders and leader sections may suit you better than what I've outlined

Seeing the fly line helps a lot when it comes to mending on the horizontal surface. Using a sighter leader goes a long way in helping the angler determine what is going on subsurface. A sighter leader is a great tool for seeing just what is happening between your indicator and your flies. Ever pick up your nymph rig to cast or perform a lift and wonder how the heck your flies got all the way over there without you knowing? With all the hidden hydraulics, that happens a lot more than we realize, especially when we're running unweighted flies. The sighter below the indicator will often show you where your flies are in relation to the indicator, so you can apply an indicator pause for the flies to catch up, or a downstream release to catch the indicator up with the flies. It's not necessary to be directly over the drifting flies all the time, but close proximity leads to fewer missed fish.

I recently was fishing the South Platte River downstream of Trumbull, Colorado in the dead of winter. Flows were low, water was gin clear, and the fish were easily visible. I opted for the eight–foot nymph leader described above as I was fishing long and lean for sure. I added a yarn/rubber–band indicator, five feet from the size four split–shot weight, for an insurance policy. My indicator was turning over perfectly by the one quarter mark of the drift, and I caught several fish on the unweighted flies, setting on a pause or twitch from the red Amnesia sighter. In many instances, the indicator never moved as I set on the sighter. This method is certainly worth a try.

Another great use of a sighter leader is to use the colored portions to suspend your nymphs at a specific level. One day, my client and I enjoyed a fine morning on Spinney Mountain Ranch near Hartsel,

Colorado, using a sighter rig under an indicator. Around lunchtime, a large thunderstorm rolled over the area while we were sitting in the comfort of my truck. After the storm passed, we made our way down to the stream roughly where we left off. Interestingly, in run after run, the fish had begun to suspend in the lower portion of the middle column. We weren't hooking up with the same regularity as before the storm, so I really had to examine what was going on. There weren't any adult flies hatching, but the fish were feeding heavily at that level. I assumed the combination of changes in water temperatures, poorer water clarity, higher flows, and the added safety of cloud cover had something to do with where and how they were feeding. That didn't matter as much as how we could get to them.

We were consistently fishing below the feeding fish, so I grabbed the red section of the sighter leader, showed my client how much of the leader I wanted below the surface, and we began to high–stick, tight–line drift right under the rod tip. My client would make a short upstream presentation, and then with a high, flat fly rod, he would drift with a certain portion of the red section of leader out of the water. In this manner, we had a way to gauge and stay consistent with putting the flies in front of the feeding fish at their levels. We caught many fish that way until it was time to depart. We never even took the indicator off, as we created collision after collision with feeding fish.

You can also employ a "sighter fly," which helps you to see where the fly is in relation to the indicator as well. A pink San Juan Worm is great for this in certain water conditions, and like the other method, offers clues as to the entire rig/drift relationship. We will later get into several mending methods, specialty casts, and rod positioning techniques that complement what we've gone over to further improve your nymph skills. The idea is to combine as much as you can to remove any luck and guesswork about the nymph drift.

All this verbiage just because you are hooking fish consistently in only one section of your drift? I know, I get it, but this will help put more fish in the bag and allow you to fish the entire drift effectively. This all goes back to those days on that still–water pond, force-feeding those bluegills and bass. If you don't put those flies in the right spot at the correct depth and speed, it's going to be a long day. Remember, rate of sink, speed of water, depth of feeding fish. Ain't no luck to it.

Just Swinging

One late February day on the South Platte near Deckers, Colorado, I was running a streamer rig, looking for willing fish. On most rivers out west, I like to run a streamer rig that uses floating fly line, about five feet of tapered leader, and a tandem brace of streamers. Typically, the leader will be a seven–and–a–half–foot 4X monofilament, cut down to the 3X section at around five feet total length. I like this configuration, because the longer leader gives ample time for the streamers to sink in our smaller, faster rivers. I had been watching a particularly large rainbow from an elevated position as she held in a dark, rock–bottomed seam for quite some time before I decided to go after her. I snuck out the way I came in to the observation spot, eased my way down the bank well out of view, and hunch–walked up the bank to a spot I thought I could do some damage.

My front streamer was a white Zonker in about a size eight. Tied off the bend and twenty inches away on 3X monofilament from the lead streamer was an Orange Blossom Special affixed by a loop knot. My plan was to perform a quarter–upstream presentation that would land in the soft water on the opposite bank, sink quickly, and, using the white Zonker as a sighter, align the drift so the second streamer cut about a foot in front of the big fish's location as it swings across the current. My swing was about three–quarters complete and I was beginning to pick up my rod tip when I noticed the unmistakable flash of a fish chasing food. She was on it, but I was out of drift. I began to strip to keep the flies moving, and with a burst of speed, she closed and ate the trailing streamer in less than a foot of water.

A strip set to my left rear pocket forced her to swirl. I could feel her weight only a few feet off the end of my fly rod, and then she inexplicably came unbuttoned! I watched as she bolted toward the center of the river, and out of desperation and a bit of frustration, I picked up and tossed a sloppy cast a handful of feet in front of her. To my dismay, she turned on the commotion of the streamers hitting the surface, and absolutely crushed the white Zonker. A solid strip set and getting her on the reel produced a very fine rainbow (pictured on the back of the book). I felt like I had nothing to do with catching her: I was just a spectator at this point. It was then I realized just how fun sight fishing with streamers could be.

Swinging streamers can be productive in many water conditions. From small upstream work to spey casting, I like it all. Most often, streamers are a means for me to scout a river looking for fish holds and feeling the seams with the drift. If you work streamers enough in plenty of different water situations, you will learn to feel the river currents as the streamers swing across them. I suggest, if you're starting out, to find two streamers you like, and fish with them in tandem over and over again on your quarter mile of river. You will begin to feel the currents, anticipate when to let it sink, when to mend, and when to strip. It simply helps make you a more complete angler.

How does the fly fishing formula fit here? Even when swinging streamers, you must be aware of speed of water, rate of sink, and depth of feeding fish. You are still striving for a fish/food collision course, although you are counting on the fish being the aggressor in most cases. You still need to get close to the fish with a lifelike presentation to elicit strikes, so there are some basic rules to follow. To start, you need to select a streamer or streamers that will give you the proper rate of sink from physical weight. This is determined in several ways, such as your skill and experience levels, characteristics of the water your fishing, and targeted fish species. For my style, skill level, and the waters I fish, I usually run an eighth-ounce dropper streamer followed (about 18 inches away) by an unweighted offering. The second in–tandem, or point, streamer will vary to account for conditions, but I will run anything from an unweighted leech to a size twelve Prince Nymph, to a size fourteen soft hackle of some sort. Again, there are no rules about what you have to throw and how you have to throw it.

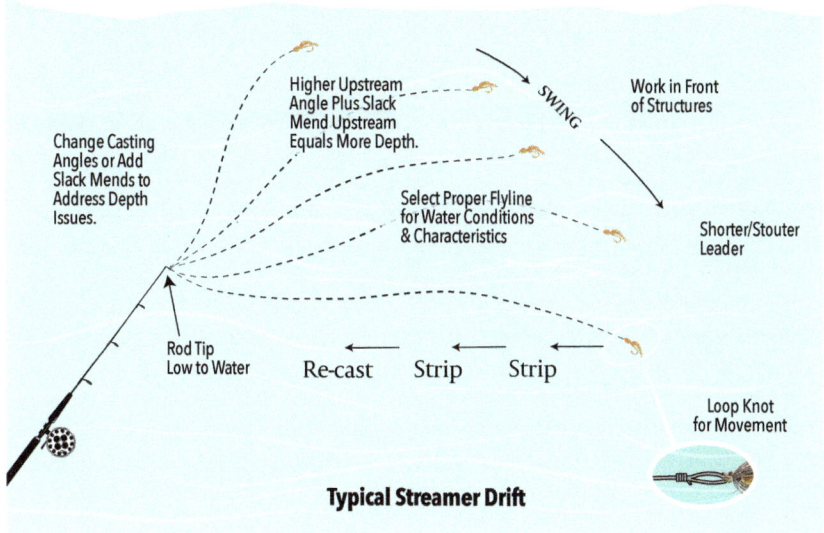

Typical Streamer Drift

If I feel as if I am not in the fish's strike zone, it's usually because I need more weight, an angle change, or to apply a few well–timed mends. "Feel" the water currents as you fish your streamers, and as usual, let the rig determine your drift/depth parameters. You can tell as your experience levels increase how your presentation is within the currents, just by observing your fly line and feeling the drag on the streamers. As you enter slower parts of the seam, you can feel less drag applied to your streamers, if you're really paying attention. Although I'll fish streamers up, down, or across the current, most of the time I'm presenting across or quarter downstream. Depending on water current and characteristics, I may need to apply a large upstream slack or pile mend to allow for additional sink before the streamers begin the swing.

Keep your rod tip low to the water, sometimes underwater, to assist in getting those streamers down. You won't always be pointing at the streamers during the drift, like when you're applying mends or when you're in the final stages of the swing, but you should practice pointing at the streamers as much as possible during the drift.

There are so many ways to present streamers, but I'll give you one scenario. Let's say you're fishing a run at least three fly rod lengths wide, moving right to left, with a soft water far edge adjacent to a faster narrow seam. Inside that seam is a nice rock line covered with walking–speed water, with another faster seam inside of that. This is a perfect scenario for throwing streamers.

Typically, I am armed with a minimum nine–foot rod, usually about a six–weight, depending on its characteristics. Nine–foot, six–weight rods most often fit the bill for our water and streamer rigs out west. My cast is usually a quarter downstream, with the flies landing as close to the edge as possible. At this juncture, my rod is high to keep the fly line off the water, preventing the faster currents from dragging it downstream before I get any sink. With the fly line under my cork hand trigger finger, and my nondominant hand holding the management loop, I slowly lower the fly rod and strip in line to get a tighter tether on the rig, which gives me more control. At this point, I usually give the rig a few cross–stream twitches, to elicit an eat, get the flies moving, or, if need be, get a visual clue as to where they are. On many occasions, these first two twitches are deadly.

Mike Connerley with a fine Brown trout picked up working the soft water in and around obstructions.

From here on out in the drift, it's a matter of feeling the water currents as you think of the fly fishing formula. If you feel you're swinging too fast or too high in the columns, apply an upstream slack or pile mend to allow for sink. If you feel you're swinging too slowly, use the management loop to your advantage and strip in line. Streamer fishing in rivers is about variation: keep attempting different retrievals at different intervals, angles, and speeds until you start finding fish. You soon begin to know when to mend, strip, and pause through on the water experience. Someday, dedicate an entire day on your quarter mile to just swinging streamers.

I remember a client from many years ago from upstate New York. His name was Bob, and I'll be darned, I can't remember his last name. He fished with me three years in a row on the South Platte near Deckers. Everyone nymphs the South Platte, but Bob wanted to throw streamers, and he was good. I learned so much from him, it was ridiculous. One thing he did that really moved a lot of fish was what he called "rocking the cradle." After the swing portion and his line had straightened, he would let go of the management loop, trap the line by pinching the cork with his index finger, then lower the flat fly rod to his side just above his knee, and rock the rod back and forth as he pointed directly at the streamers. This forced the streamers to move upstream and then fall back, mimicking a wounded fish. Sometimes he would rock the cradle for fifteen to twenty seconds as we talked, slightly changing the downstream rod angle, and then, wham! Bob also liked to put a stick–on foam indicator four feet above his first streamer to assist in strike detection, and he was the first person that I witnessed jigging streamers Czech–style under his rod tip. I learned a lot from Bob.

I marveled at his ability to move fish directly under his rod tip while jigging a streamer off the bottom as it drifted downstream. We employed lead head jigs with various streamer patterns copied to perform the jig. Bob would cast a rod length upstream at about a sixty–degree angle, suck in line with his management loop until the fly contacted the bottom, then with a flat fly rod about chest high, simply lift the fly a couple of inches, and drop it as he slowly worked downstream. He could feel the jig bouncing on the bottom as he gently led it downstream. At the end of the drift, a slow lift was always factored in.

There are countless ways to satisfy the fly fishing formula. Whether you're swinging streamers, nymphing, dry–dropping, or strictly dry fly fishing, the formula is always in play. Your goal is to force fish to eat or get out of the way. You can do this even if you're not throwing the perfect flies, if your presentation is solid. Remember, it's all about speed of the water, rate of sink, and depth of feeding fish.

That's Fly

I WAS PREPARING for a guide trip one day not too long ago, in the fly shop on a busy summer morning. As I was zipping back and forth between the wader and boot room, the licensing machine, and my clients, I overheard a couple of twentysomethings at the fly bins discussing their options. This was clearly a team effort, as one guy held the fly cup and the other was busy poking through the bins in search of the perfect fly. I couldn't resist and stopped to offer a bit of assistance.

"Can I help you guys out a bit?" I asked.

"No, no," the one with the cup in his hands said. Then he said, and not to me, "We have a couple with beads, a couple that are 'sposed to float, and a big purple one: think we got it."

Just then, the other guy looks up from the bins and says, "Oh, wait, we need some with legs."

"Okay, guys, sounds like you've got it licked, have a great day," I replied as I hustled away.

Fly selection should be much more than a buffet–line approach. There's more than a bit of science that goes into picking the proper fly for the situations presented.

Some folks have said that selecting a fly is nothing more than guesswork, and that couldn't be further from the truth. Selecting flies comes down to observation and data. The guesswork creeps in when you aren't confident your flies are at the proper depths, or if the fish aren't actively feeding. Still, even if you're not sure where and on what insects the fish are feeding, if you follow the systematic approach and have "ballpark flies," there's a good chance you'll move a few fish. "Ballpark" flies are representations of the main insect classifications that concern us as fly fishers. Most often, they aren't perfectly accurate, but are close enough to be in the "ballpark". Even if you don't hook up, you can most often walk away from a run that you fished, knowing that you fished it well. Before we get into fly selection, let's continue to build a foundational block and close any communication gap we may have.

There are four main classifications of insects that we are interested in as fly fishers: mayflies, caddis, midges, and stoneflies. Basically, that's it, but you need to be able to recognize the stages of these insects as well: nymph, emerger, pupa stage, dun, adult, spinner, and spent. You should be able to recognize each and, more importantly, reach in your fly box and pull out its match. Plus, we will throw in terrestrials, bait or immature fish, scuds and leeches to round out our selection process and our fly boxes. Your fly box may look different than mine beyond the four main classes of insects. That's geographical, historical, and personal preference legit.

You don't have to be able to recite all the Latin insect names according to their taxonomic hierarchy to be able to accurately fill your fly box. You only need to be able to observe the fly the fish are eating, where they're eating it, and how they're eating it to pick out its imposter. It's easier than it sounds, believe me.

With so much information at our fingertips, an angler can get a grip on entomology in short order by clipping off the top of the learning curve in various ways. One way is to look for historical and seasonal data that contains insect names and the months of the year they are prevalent on certain waters. These hatch charts are incredibly easy to find for your particular water, whether you live out east or out west. Doing simple searches, you'll find hatch charts that give you a solid idea of what flies to expect at what times of the year, and are usually very accurate. Although very helpful, the average hatch chart doesn't show you colors or sizes of the naturals; however, historical data gives you an overview of the yearly hatches on your river, while the seasonal data concerns what bugs will hatch each month and how various hatches overlap. Conditional hatching data is a day–to–day thing observable as you stand knee–deep in the river. Conditional data, like sizes and colors, only accurately comes from game–time conditions and observations.

For example, on the Eagle River in Colorado in April, we historically should see Baetis, also known as Blue–Winged Olives (BWOs), some early caddis, and possibly some little black stoneflies and midges. Seasonally speaking, I will concentrate our rigs on the caddis and BWOs, while adjusting to environmental and observable conditional factors as the day progresses. How do I know this? Because I have filled many pages of my journal with exactly that information. It's all backed up by data. This data becomes my historical information on my river, specifically my quarter mile of river, but it doesn't end there.

The Eagle River is over seventy miles long, and I fish the majority of it as it comes down from the high peaks, rolls along the I–70 corridor, and eventually dumps into the Colorado River. As it gathers more water from several tributaries, it changes not only in size but also in structure, gradient, and insect species. Therefore, as you apply what you've learned on one section to another section, things become less clear and less compatible the farther away from your quarter mile you go. This is because of several factors, the most important being water temperatures.

The longer the main stem of a river, freestone, or tailwater, and the more diverse geography it cuts and elevation it loses, the more bug life will differ from its origin to its end. So hatch charts are a good tool to get you started, but not the best. For example, caddis may be popping on the lower stretches of a river, but are weeks away from hatching on the upper stretches, because of water, sun angles, and day time temperatures. Also, just for caddis, there are dozens of species spread out along the river length. How can you possibly know this before you make the trek to your favorite river to hit the caddis hatch? Well, with the availability of social media and your good old–fashioned fly shops at your disposal, there is hope. Hope that extends beyond a hatch chart, hope that comes from knowledge observed first–hand from other anglers.

As you spend a day fishing on the river, take a moment to write down a few tidbits about flows, water clarity, water temperatures, and of course, insect hatches observed. You're now building your own historical and seasonal data, which go well beyond a simple hatch chart. Just for fun, start to document what flies the fish liked best, at what temperatures they ate those flies, where the majority of the fish were when they ate, and how you were rigged. I will convert a few of you yet. Journaling is the key!

Breaking Down the Bugs: Caddis Anyone?

To make sure we are speaking the same language and building off the same foundation, let's perform a quick overview of the main classes of the insects we rely on. Let's begin with caddis. Caddis are those flies that flutter around like moths over a river. They are easily recognizable by the way they flutter about, but the obscurity is what lies below the hood, under the tent–shaped wings. Anglers should get into the habit of capturing an individual of two and flipping it over to look at the abdomen color and length. I've seen underbellies of tan, green, black, brown, and orange: they all come off the Eagle River at various times of the year. If your hatch chart or other data source says there are supposed to be caddis coming off or hatching and you're not seeing them, then walking the banks and shaking bushes before a day of fishing can pay off, as you should scare a few off the branches. They're usually around if the hatch chart calls for it, but most mornings, they are hard to find, since they are most active later in the day.

Many think that all caddis are alike; that couldn't be further from the truth. Caddis are very diverse in their emergence, home-building, and egg–laying behaviors. They often give fly fishers fits because of the many ways you can fish them. Sometimes, fish become dialed in on one species of caddis in one stage of its life. If you're concentrating on drifting adults and the fish are dialed into the intriguing act of a female dapping eggs on the surface, you are most likely in for a long day. When fly fishing caddis imitations, you'd better be versatile enough to match not only the hatch, but also the stages and somewhat goofy behaviors. I have been on the river many times during a good caddis hatch, wondering why we weren't just tearing up the surface action. Sure, there were a few fish slapping the surface as the mature adults fluttered off it, but we weren't getting the action on dead drifting or skating our flies like I imagined. More often than not, the fish in this instance are eating the caddis aggressively; they're just doing the work subsurface, where they are mostly unobservable. Many times, imitating a caddis pupa as it emerges and swings through the columns is what the fish are truly keyed in to. There are many patterns that will cover the emergence just fine.

Caddis aren't like mayflies in their life cycle. They begin as larvae, pupate, then become adults. The larvae often build their own cases: some use rocks, sand, twigs, or even build their own case of silk. Some build nets they use to trap other insects, others simply cruise the bottom without any net or case. When the larvae mature and are ready to pupate, many of the species often begin to drift long distances in the various water columns. Some hatch by breaking through the surface film and quickly flying off, while others skitter across the water surface to the bank to crawl out and hatch. This behavior really gets the attention of hungry trout. When you combine hungry fish, somewhat erratic movement across the water, and a quick flight off the water surface after hatching, you can see why there are plenty of splashy rises when caddis are hatching.

Most of my time, whether I'm guiding or fishing during a caddis hatch, is spent running soft hackles. Sure, I like to catch fish on the surface with Elk Hair Caddis, but if I really want to catch fish, and I do, I go to my favorite soft hackles to get the job done. Before the hatch begins, I will run my inline nymph rig with three flies. My first dropper will be an attractor of some sort, usually a San Juan Worm. My San Juans are tied on Tiemco R200 size 10 hooks, with a full one–and–a–half–inch section of tan chenille. The chenille is affixed using UTC 140 Fluorescent Pink. Folks that fish with me know there is usually a worm as an attractor in the nymph rig. It's there to attract attention, be eaten, and add versatility to the nymph rig. We will get into versatility later.

Below the worm will be a Soft–hackled Pheasant Tail tied in the color of the caddis hatching. After that, I'll tie off the eye of the hook to my next offering. If you're fishing a two–bug rig, you can use the soft hackle for your attractor, then drop your next favorite bug below it. For spring caddis, I tie my softies with a plastic gold-colored bead (refer to recipe). My usual body color for them is either natural pheasant tail or black-dyed pheasant tail. For the spring, I will run them in a size 16 or 18, but my records indicate the size 18 outperforms the size 16 (in my area) about two to one. My soft hackles are tied "spider-like," with two good wraps of a slightly over-long partridge feather. I like to extend the soft hackle when wet about a quarter of the shank length past the hook bend. The soft hackle has been in my fly box since I was a kid, and has been a staple in my nymph rigs for over ten years. The softie is a lively bug, and mimics a pupating caddis very well. It's not flashy or conceited. It just works.

Black Soft-hackled Pheasant Tail #16-18 Umpqua 2488 or MFC #16 7077, Body-Black Pheasant Tail with small Gold Wire wrap, Head-plastic or tungsten small gold bead, Wing-1 ½ wraps Hungarian Partridge, Thread-Red 8/0 Uni.

One day I was guiding a single client on the Eagle. We were having a good day finding fish in several slots at various levels. Our trip was almost over when we came to the head of a run. This particular spot is not the easiest to fish because it's where the river really narrows and drops hard over a protruding shelf. This creates a large pool abruptly below the shelf that has all kinds of crazy hydraulics; therefore, you are best served to nymph it with plenty of weight to get those bugs down quickly. I remember pinching tungsten putty onto the rig for my client, just above the weight, and sliding the indicator up about six inches to account for the aforementioned. Even though you're almost on top of the run, the fish can't see you through the depth and turbulence. It's a tricky presentation, because you have to cast into raging water in an attempt to come off the shelf correctly, peacefully, and quickly.

After getting my client set up and in position, I moved upstream of him about five feet, and got on my hands and knees to peer into the gin–clear water below the foam, the bubbles, and crisscrossing seams. I could see several fish happily suspended in feeding lanes. There were a few dandies in there.

"Okay," I said, "Give me a good shot up on the shelf, and get the line off the water quickly so the weight can do its job."

His first presentation was perfect. I could clearly see the flies as they came off the shelf and attained full depth. I could easily see the size 18 black Soft–hackled Pheasant Tail cruising and flexing in the water. The undulating of the soft–hackle Hungarian partridge was too much for an 18–inch rainbow to resist: I watched that fish smoothly swim a foot ahead and suck that fly in. I didn't say a word; I was too caught up in the moment. The fish had the fly in its mouth for a solid two seconds and spat it out without the indicator even moving. I was just getting ready to relay the events to my client, when to my surprise, that same fish turned, chasing that soft hackle downstream, and absolutely hammered it going away.

My client, who had missed all of the underwater excitement, said, "Here's one!" to which I replied, "My friend, you just never know."

That's the beauty of fishing during caddis season: you can get away with your flies dragging and swinging, because caddis are underwater acrobats. Basically, you can fish poorly and still catch fish because of the nature of the hatch. From deep–water nymphing to swinging suspended flies to top water presentations, fish are looking for movement and vitality during caddis season, and it's easy to capitalize on that. Even when there are adults present and fish feeding madly on top, I prefer to run a mini–rig at them that has a softie or other pupa imitation, such as Larry Kingrey's Ice Caddis, as the initial dropper. The fish will often eat the big indicator bug because they are already looking up, but the real magic occurs subsurface. I often carry a double–dry rig on another rod during this time for fun, but the bread is buttered on that soft hackle.

When carrying a spare rod rigged for caddis on top, I'm fairly picky as to how I set this rig up. The first thing I do is make sure I'm running 5X monofilament leader to the Elk Hair Caddis. I have found that 5X leader is a good option for tying off to the dropper, because it is strong enough to withstand the prolific takes you can get with this fly, it turns over well, and it's fine enough not to be overly obtrusive. Of course, there are other patterns of adult caddis out there, but this is what I prefer. I'm going to go out of my way to ensure I have the correct body length and color. I can use data sources to help in this endeavor, but with so many species of caddis where I fish, I'd rather take a minute, shake a few bushes, and get a good look at the real thing. Once I'm satisfied I have the correct body color and length, I'll tie on my first fly.

My preferred dropper off the Elk Hair will probably catch a few of you by surprise. I like to drop a dark Olive Sparkle Dun behind the first fly. I am especially fond of Craig Matthews' pattern of that fly. Typically, during caddis season, there are also BWOs present and hatching, maybe not in the same numbers, but they are there. I find dropping the Sparkle Dun (size 20), twenty inches behind the Elk Hair with 5X or 6X monofilament connecting the two helps me move the most fish. I choose monofilament tippet between the two flies because it floats better than fluorocarbon, and that helps keep that small dun pattern floating. Actually, my records show that this rig catches more fish on the Sparkle Dun than the Elk Hair. My theory is that there are so many caddis fluttering, floating, and popping off the water that a nice peaceful meal on the BWO pattern is welcomed. By the way, the reason I run a size 20 sparkle dun is because the natural BWO that is coming off at this time is a size 18. My rule of thumb when fishing a dun pattern is to drop a size from the hatching natural. We'll get into this more when we talk about mayflies.

A bit more about the versatility of an Elk Hair Caddis. There are times when the females of certain caddis species dive sub-surface to deposit eggs. The fish truly key in on this behavior, as the bug is mostly defenseless. I will use a regular caddis dry fly under an indicator, dropped below a dry, or in a mini–rig to match that behavior. Really concentrate on the swing portion of the drift, as the takes can be prolific. I will also take an Elk Hair that has seen some action and is a bit on the rugged side, grab the wing, and splay it out to the sides to give a spent appearance. Watch the water closely and, when the flies begin to fall to the surface spent, get yourself into this game as soon as possible.

I need to say a bit more about soft hackles. There is a soft hackle in my rig somewhere when I'm nymphing and dry dropping. No exceptions. Heck, I even throw one behind a large streamer at times. I'm a soft–hackle junkie, because they can mimic everything from a diving egg–laying caddis to an emerging mayfly. Typically, my soft hackle ties are not weighted, and they only carry a weighted bead until the 4th of July. After the 4th, I tie all my ties with thread heads because I feel the fish are getting bead–shy or bead–fatigued. I know that sounds obscure, but I can honestly feel comfortable stating that, and it drives how I tie my flies. No bead flies after the 4th of July. There are instances which I will tie gold or black tungsten beads on my soft hackles, and it's usually for high water when the added weight is welcome, or when I'm fishing still waters, such as lakes.

I used to guide pheasant hunters with my two German shorthair pointers during the winter months. For the most part, this kept me off the river from mid-November to the end of February. One February not too long ago, after a fairly large chunk of time spent in the fields and not on the river, I was able to get back on and guide the Eagle River. The guide I worked with knows his way around a fly-tying vice for sure. Having not been on the river in several weeks, I rigged my clients with my confidence nymph rig that had a size 20 black Soft-hackled Pheasant Tail in its customary second position in the in-line three fly rig. After going over a few technical and mechanical have-tos with our clients, we broke into groups of two clients per guide and spread out a bit in one section. Within the first dozen casts, my two anglers had landed three fish and turned a few more.

This prompted my colleague to yell, "Hey fish, Redford's back in town! You may want to lay off the soft hackles!" One of the best compliments I ever had.

The set on a swung fly can be confusing to the angler, and can result in many missed fish because of the mechanics of the set. More often than not, you're going to feel the fish take the fly as it swings through and across the water. The swung soft-hackle take is typically in the last quarter of the drift, therefore your line is tight or close to it. If the water is flowing from your left to your right, and the flies are swinging in the last quarter of the drift to your right, your set should be low across the water to your right. When setting on swung fly drifts, simply think to continue your set to the downstream drift side, instead of abruptly lifting the fly rod up when you feel the take. This allows the fish a chance to eat the fly, and then turn downstream as it prepares to move back to its holding area.

Drowning soft hackles is part of my program, and I'm comfortable fishing them year-round. The only things that change are the colors and sizes of the fly. They are basic, not a lot of flash, just a body wrapped in copper wire and a couple of wraps of a slightly longer than usual Hungarian partridge feather. Sometimes I'll add a "hot spot" of fluorescent pink UTC Thread 70 behind the bead; otherwise, my finishing thread is 8/0 Dark Red. My statistics tell me that I use "hot spots" with most success during runoff, which is understandable because of water clarity, and in September. The September statistics have me a bit confused, but I'm sure there are several factors that make that my second most successful month with "hot spot" pheasant tails. Probably something to do with lower sun angles, less light permeating the water, spawn and winter preparation, and the wane in the bug life for about two weeks. Sometimes you don't need to know and should just go with it.

Most soft hackles are very durable, and actually fish better as they get a bit torn up with the more fish you catch. Here's my basic approach to fishing soft hackles for most of our Western rivers and streams:

- Black with Gold Bead—February Through May (runoff)
- Tan Dubbed or Natural Pheasant Tail with No or Glass Bead—July Through September
- Orange and Black with Gold Bead or Red Thread Head—October to January

I'm not against any other caddis larva or pupa imitations out there. I just know what works for my program, and I'm comfortable with it. I've used probably every fly out there when it comes to caddis, but prefer to stay with what my data supports. Picking flies requires confidence. We all have our confidence flies. That is not to say we won't try new bugs, but most often, we go back to the old producers. My confidence flies haven't changed in years, and my data continues to support them. It takes a lot for accomplished anglers to supplant a fly that's been a producer for years. I find old flies are like baseballs: you either lose them, wear them out, or retire them to a place of honor.

A Soft-Hackled Pheasant tail fooled this buck Rainbow Trout.
Soft hackles are not only very effective, but patterns such as this one are easy ties.

MAYFLIES

Remember when I said not to get too hung up on insect names and taxonomy? Well, this is a perfect time to take that to heart. Mayflies are very common in this country, and have thousands of species. Not only that, but there is some confusion as to what to call, and how to define, a certain species that we as fly fishers depend upon. I'm talking about the Blue–winged Olive or BWO. These little mayflies are our foundation as fly fishers, but aren't always "blue–winged" or "olive." Some folks refer to them as Baetis, some call them baetids, but for the purposes of our discussion, let's simplify and call them all BWOs. Their behavior patterns are so similar that lumping them together is much simpler than trying to break it all down as to which insect goes in which class. It's much easier to be able to recognize a BWO and match its size and color from your fly box than to try to recite its

Latin name. Suffice it to say that these bugs come in many variations during different times of the year and in different sections of a river.

The BWO nymphs are torpedolike swimmers, and it's not unusual for them to show off their swimming skills and move from one part of the river to the next. The nymph color is dark brown to olive, with shades of gray at times. The most prolific hatches I see occur between 43–and 47–degree water temps. It's not unusual for me to tell clients to hang on because we need just a few more degrees before a place lights up with a BWO hatch and aggressive fish. This is why carrying a thermometer can pay huge dividends in helping you stay ahead of the hatch. We have talked at length about how knowledge and experience can help you predict what's about to happen on the river. It's not guesswork. Taking the time to read and document temperatures, times, and hatches is as easy as it is effective.

You've got to be careful trying to mimic mayflies: they are similar, yet can be vastly different. Let's look at the nymphs, for example. Some are swimmers, some clingers that cling to the bottom, some are stout–bodied crawlers, and others are burrowers that dig into the substrate. This information is only a fraction of a second away, and is critical when you tie or buy flies for your water. On the waters I guide and fish on, the main mayflies are the BWO, the Pale Morning Dun (PMD), various Drakes, and the Tricorythodes or Trico. Sure, we have others, and variations of the ones I listed, but these are the go–to in my area. Your flies may vary in size and species where you live, so it's important to do your homework and dial in the flies and behaviors of your area to develop your go–tos.

My favorite nymph for fishing BWOs is a simple Pheasant Tail in sizes 18–20. Of course, you want to match your bug size on your quarter mile to the natural, so your sizes may vary. I like a slim profile nymph tie, in the spirit of a Sawyer pattern, without any weight added. Brown thread all the way on my nymphs and emergers, because I am capitalizing on the colors of the naturals at those same stages. I can honestly say that I haven't tied on any other color but brown for my

BWO nymphs and emergers for at least five years. I easily go through a spool and a half of 6/0 Dark Brown thread a year, by just tying size 18–20 BWO nymphs and emerger patterns. I don't tie professionally: these are my guide flies.

Speaking of guide flies, I was showing a couple of accomplished tiers a couple of bugs I had been doing very well with on the river. After looking at them, one of the gentlemen said, "Those are nice guide flies."

At first, that comment took me aback, but since then, I smile when I think about it, because he was exactly right. My flies aren't beautiful: they don't catch fishermen, they are designed to catch fish. Folks could take my patterns and make them prettier, but they won't catch any more fish. My ties do impressions. I want ease of tying, simple durable patterns, versatility, and a triggering mechanism in the pattern. Therefore, I use a lot of razor foam in my ties. It provides the trigger or "hot spot" a bit of buoyancy so I can fish it anywhere in the water columns, including the film, and it provides the impression or profile I am looking for with my BWO flies.

Butt Crack Baetis Hook-#18-20 MFC 7077 or #18-20 MFC 7125, Tail-6 Hungarian Partridge fibers, Body-6/0 or 8/0 Uni Brown Thread with copper or gold Small Wire wrap, Thorax-.5 Razor Foam white wrapped over Rusty UV Ice Dub and RSII Pearl Braid wing tip, Head-Thread wrap.

Pictured is the Butt Crack Baetis (BCB). This pattern is about four generations old, and is finally where I want it to be. It's been catching me tons of fish for years, but a few final tweaks have made this fly special. This emerger pattern has what I want in a fly. First off, it's simple. Second, it's deadly during Trico, BWO, or Psuedo BWO hatches. It's a guide fly. What this bug emulates is that stage where the nymph is beginning to split the exoskeleton. This stage and the dun stage are when the BWO is so vulnerable to predation. As the nymph begins to advance into the emerger phase, it splits above the thorax in preparation of exiting the exoskeleton. The razor foam pullover is one piece, split and tied in to represent that split. After tying in the razor foam, tie in a section of Pearl or Rootbeer braid. Then dub over that. Once that's done and your thread is advanced to the eye, pull over the razor foam to form the split, tie off, and thread from the head. Trim the braid above the split fairly close to the foam, but make sure it's visible. The Hungarian partridge tail fibers should be tied to about the same length as the body, but if they're a bit longer, they won't detract from the effectiveness of the fly. This fly has been picked up by Montana Fly Company and will be available in early 2018.

I've heard it said over the years that mayflies actually coordinate the place on the river and the time to hatch because of safety in numbers. Since they are so vulnerable in the emergence and dun phases, there's more than a bit of sense to this. Not all mayflies emerge the way BWOs do, some (a very few) actually become a dun subsurface and float to the top to hatch. The dun stage, or the stage where most mayflies sit on the water's surface after emergence, is a very important stage to fly fishers. Before the dun flies off to molt one more time into a spinner, it floats on the surface, preparing to take flight. During a hatch, take a minute to get low and look across the water surface. You'll see many tiny sailboats on the surface. Always makes me think of America's Cup sailboat races.

Now is a good time to discuss dry fly set mechanics. This is probably one of the areas of guiding that brings me great joy and great frustration. I love watching folks set on dry fly eats on top, love their actions and excitement, but there are times it can be frustrating, because we miss so many fish when throwing dry flies! It's tough because of the difficulty in seeing the dry fly, timing, and determining the direction of the set. The anticipation when watching your well–mended dry fly floating into the feeding zone can be high–octane, and when you get a fish to rise on your fly and it eats, sometimes the sets are much less than perfect. I have watched folks (including myself) set too early, too late, too soft, too hard, and in the wrong direction.

Setting on a dry fly eat in fast moving water is probably the easiest and most productive when it comes to hooking fish consistently on the surface. You need to simply react to the take in a high over the downstream shoulder motion to straighten out the line. Fish in faster water usually use the quick simple rise to eat facing upstream and, after eating, quickly return to their original holding position. Because this movement is done quickly, the fish has less time to spit your fly, and often hooks itself as it quickly turns and descends to original holds. Fish in slower glides are much more difficult to time, eat at a slower pace, and will display many types of rises, including the compound and complex, which we will discuss in the next chapter.

Top water eaters in slower water present more of a challenge because you have to be aware of which direction they are swimming when they eat so you can effectively set "against" the fish, and it is difficult to get your timing as fish eat in slower water. Setting "against" the fish simply means you set in the opposite direction the fish is facing, from its head to its tail. When you're long–distance casting to surface feeders, this is not often easy to see, so you may miss fish and not even know why. At close proximity, where you can see the direction of the fish feeding on your fly, simply set against it, be it upstream or downstream. The idea is to try to hook the fish as it begins to descend with your fly, but you can't wait too long, since the fish will quickly figure out your fly is an imposter and spit it out. Sometimes, when clients are amped for the dry fly set with anticipation, I'll have them say "One Mississippi" out loud after the take and before they can set. This sometimes helps in the timing, not always, but it sure is comical.

Setting on a fly that you can pick out of the masses of other real insects is a large part of the battle. Often, I'll see a fish eat our dry fly and say, "Lift!," only to have my client say, "I didn't see it." There are a couple of things you can do right away to help you see your flies amongst the masses. One is to put a highly visible post or wing section on them when you tie them or purchase them that way. This often helps greatly, and doesn't seem to spook fish in the least. Another way to help find your flies is to over–cast, or cast beyond your target seam, then lift your rod and slide the flies toward you and into the intended seam. This simple move allows you to find and track your flies easily.

The take on a mayfly dun is not nearly as splashy and prolific as when a trout slams a caddis or stonefly. The take is usually nothing more than a casual sip, with just the fish's nose exposed. We will get more into reading trout that are elevating and/or breaking the surface later, but for now, suffice it to say, trout can lazily feed on mayfly duns. This point in the hatch usually takes place on calmer, walking–speed water on the glide sections of a run. Therefore, an angler has more than a few options as to how to fish it and what flies to employ.

When I find myself in this situation, usually I've already been fishing this run, either nymphing it or mini–rigging it. As the water temperatures rise, the mayflies begin to pop off the surface. I've probably been doing fairly well with a BCB or Pheasant Tail, but other options are available as well, such as Craven's Juju series or Chung's RSII, or Juan Ramirez's Slim Shady. Whichever bugs you choose pre–hatch, just make sure you have colors, sizes, and profiles matched. Here's where folks get the impression that mayflies coordinate times and places to hatch, because very often the water is quickly covered with duns, with plenty of adults in the air. I prefer to think conditions guide them to hatch like this. Water temperatures, sun angles, cloud cover, humidity, air and water speeds all play a role in the hatch. The fact that hatches can be prolific is Mama Nature's way of protecting the species by making sure some breeding goes on, while providing safety in numbers. Either way, it's a blast to fish the phases of the hatch.

For fishing into the teeth of this hatch, I will either double–dry rig it, mini–rig it, skinny–rig it (an obscure technique, so we will talk later about this), dry–drop it, or all four. Usually depends on how much fun my clients want to have. To double–dry fish a BWO hatch, I will run a size 18 (or the size of the natural) Parachute Adams, followed by 20 inches of 5x or 6x monofilament tippet to a size 20 Sparkle Dun. It doesn't matter if I'm fishing a BWO, Trico, Drake or PMD hatch. All I need to do is match colors to the patterns and run the natural size adult or spinner, followed by the dun a size smaller. I've been running this rig for many years and it catches a lot of fish, usually on the dun pattern, but it can cover a couple of phases of the hatch, so it's wise to keep the Parachute Adams in the rig. Not only does it help you see the dun pattern, the fish will begin to take it more often once you've worked the run for a bit and the females begin to come back to lay eggs.

The Sparkle Dun can be tied to imitate a PMD or Drake, among others. For attacking the fish on the surface during a PMD hatch, I'll throw a Pale Morning Dun Thorax followed by a PMD Sparkle Dun a size smaller than the natural. I see a handful of different drakes hatching on the waters I fish, and I'm always quick to switch out when I see the first few adults, because the fish are always on them when they're present. I like Schmidt's Green Drake or Furimsky's Green Drake trailed by the Sparkle Dun. A drake hatch is always a great time, as the surface bite can be prolific.

There are times you should employ a single dry fly connected to a long leader. When you have that big, mature fish that's tucked into a tricky spot, feeding very subtly on unsuspecting adults, it's time to get into stealth mode. Depending on the situation, fish location, length of cast, fish size, and fish maturity, I will choose the leader length and diameter. It's not unusual to throw an eleven–foot leader that drops down to 6x diameter with a single bug affixed. I certainly don't want that fish seeing anything but the fly, and I choose to run a single fly in these cases because I think there is almost imperceptible drag applied to the flies tied in tandem. No matter how good the drift is, when you are running tandem flies in this situation, experienced fish often ignore you. The majority of the time, I throw tandem dry flies on eight and nine–foot 5x leaders, but sometimes conditions dictate otherwise and you have to become a ninja.

The mini–rig is fun to employ during the hatch with the typical indicator bug up top, and yes, it's not unusual to have it eaten, followed by a size 18 tan or olive Soft–hackle with a BCB or Chocolate Thunder below that. The Chocolate Thunder is a nickname I gave one of my longtime favorite flies. It's a Solitude pattern that's called the Brown RSII Foam Wing. Great fly. It should be somewhere in your box. Of course, you can run your favorite flies in any of these rigs: I'm simply showing you my program, with the flies I trust. I also will run a size 18 BlackSoft–hackled Pheasant Tail in the mini–rig in these situations because, don't forget, there's usually a caddis hatch not far off.

Brown Foam-back Emerger–AKA Chocolate Thunder Hook–#18-20 MFC 7125, Tail-6 Hungarian Partridge fibers, Body-6/0 or 8/0 Uni Brown Thread with copper or gold Small Wire wrap, Thorax-Sparkle Tinsel wrap behind square cut Razor foam 1.0mm, Head-Thread wrap.

Probably my most effective way to fish a mayfly hatch is a simple dry drop rig; however, my dropper fly is fished in the film about 20 inches behind the dry on 5 or 6x. I will use the same Parachute Adams patterns as my lead fly, again making sure that the color and size is correct, and I will follow this with one of my favorite drowned, spent, or crippled patterns. This fly is called the Crazy Lady, and she is a very versatile little bug. Drowning can occur anytime in the hatch window. The spent stage is after mating, and the crippled insects usually appear throughout the main hatch, so the Crazy Lady has it covered. I fish this fly with several methods from subsurface nymphing in a dead drift to applying floatant to the tippet within a couple of inches of the fly fishing in the film behind a dry fly. In the heat of the hatch, swinging this fly through the riffles on a short line can be deadly. That's why she's crazy. The large piece of razor foam helps with buoyancy and provides a contrasting hot–spot, and, I think, when dead drifted, it acts as a rudder and gives this fly extra movement.

As always, there are more than a few options when it comes to tying or purchasing flies. That's the beauty of the sport, you can personalize it and participate. Sometimes I will tie the Crazy Lady with Rootbeer D–rib for the body, when I'm looking to create a few that I just want to dead drift or swing. I have used many different hen hackles for the wings, including Brahma dun, hen pheasant, and blue hen, but I always make sure the tail and wings match. At this point you may be wondering why, with so many colors of razor foam available, I predominately use white. I think white outperforms all the other colors when it comes to mayfly ties. The stark contrast of white foam against a dark brown body is very compelling in ordinary light, and have you looked at white razor foam under UV lighting?

Crazy Lady Hook-#18-20 MFC 7077 or #18-20 MFC 7125, Tail-6 Hungarian Partridge fibers, Body-6/0 Uni Brown Thread with copper or gold Small Wire wrap, Thorax-.5 Razor Foam white wrapped over Rusty Brown UV Ice Dub and Split feather Light Blue Hen, Head- Extended Razor foam and thread wrap.

When the hatch is waning and the spinners are beginning to fall spent, sometimes the same day, sometimes the next day, it is time to change your Parachute Adams to a brown or rust body to take advantage of the dying spinner's body colors. Not all mayflies turn the rusty color; for example, female Trico spinner bodies turn gray and the males turn black. Therefore, you have to be supremely aware of the characteristics of all stages of mayflies on the water you fish. If the fish are coming up to the spinners, I like to run the proper spinner imitation with the Crazy Lady trailing, because the brown body covers many color options. As for spent mayflies, there are many patterns out there that represent fallen or spent insects. I always tie or look for patterns with splayed wings and lower floating profiles. I often fish these on longer nine–foot thin leaders and fish them as a single. It's more fun that way as you try to put your spent within the masses of spents to a specific feeding fish.

Once you fish through enough mayfly hatches to get the sequence of events figured out, specific stages become less obscure. Once the stages are figured out, you can augment that information by selecting the proper mayfly offering for that stage, in the proper size, profile, and color. Once you have that figured out, you determine the best way to present the flies, using various techniques and mechanics. I think a lot of folks miss the pure beauty of a mayfly hatch and its stages because they get too amped about all the flies that can be surrounding them. The beauty of this hatch, as any other, is to get ahead of it. Anticipate and predict what's going to happen next and when, and select the proper fly and technique to get it done. This hatch is truly hidden in plain view, but shouldn't be.

STONEFLIES

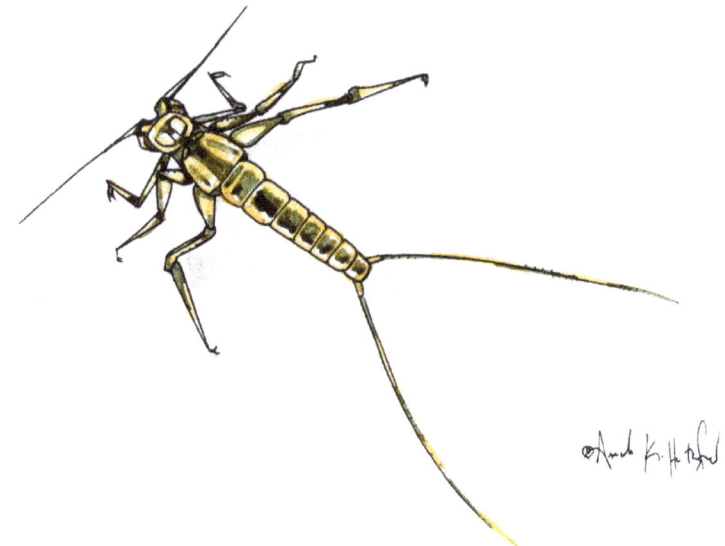

Stoneflies, Mama Nature's underwater scorpions. I rely on stoneflies, those prehistoric insects that drive trout wild, to bring me plenty of action year–round. The stoneflies I observe on the waters I frequent are anywhere from a half an inch to an inch and a half long, and they all look like something that crawled out of an old science-fiction movie. These creepy–crawlies can live years underwater; many prey on other insects. Stoneflies are badass.

As always, one must look to historical and seasonal data to discern which species of stoneflies inhabit your waters. In Colorado, both on the western slope and the Front Range waters I guide and fish, I am ultimately concerned with four different species of stonefly. I rely on the nymph at certain times of the year and the adult at other times, but it is very clear that I count on this water scorpion to help me put fish in the bag. We'll look at smaller and bigger varieties, but make no mistake, the size of the stonefly doesn't dictate its importance.

The smallest stone I know of in the waters I fish is the little brown stone. These guys are 3/8 to a ½ inch long where I work, and come off at the exact time I'm tired of drowning midges in the winter. They usually start to hatch in February, and I've seen them as late as mid–May, depending on the year. Like their larger cousins, these little stones begin to migrate to the water's edge shortly before crawling out and hatching. This "terrestrial hatch" is very important to anglers, because the fish follow the migration to the river edge. The little brown stones lose many in their ranks during this crawling migration, and fly fishers can take advantage of this phenomenon and catch fish on the nymph along the edges, as the fish are beginning to shake the winter blues and look for larger meals.

Often, I have folks tell me in February and early March that they are really hammering fish on black RSIIs. I'll ask them why that fly is working so well, and I have yet to have one of them tell me it's because the little brown stones are hatching. These are the same folks that wonder why we're catching fish in March on a size 16 Black Elk Hair Caddis pattern. In other words, these little guys are often overlooked, and folks are lucking into a few patterns that work and don't really know why. Consult your local hatch chart this winter, and look for little brown, almost black, stoneflies running on the snow banks nearest you, and use this little bug to get you through the winter blues. Let's graduate in size to my favorite stonefly, the yellow sally. As their little cousin, most "sallies" migrate to the water's edge to hatch from their nymphal shuck. Some, however, hatch just like a mayfly and emerge through the surface film. And like fish are inclined to do, they follow this migration, and crush the flies poking through the film. The nymphs are ½ to ¾ inch long depending on the hatch near you, and brown to yellowish brown in color. The adults typically have yellow to yellow/green bodies with a hint of red on the abdomen and up along the back. These little adults can really move quickly, and I've looked like a fool more than once trying to capture one off my body. They disappear and reappear incredibly fast, making it hard to get a good picture of them. The females deposit eggs by dipping their abdomens several times, and eventually fall spent. Both of those activities are of interest to trout and must be capitalized upon.

Enter the Yellow Soozie. Many years ago, I was fishing the Eagle River with a couple of my favorite clients and people. The yellow sally stones were really active that day both in migration and egg–laying. I had been developing a fly for just this occasion for quite some time, and predicting this may happen because of environmental conditions coupled with my data, I had the fly in each client's nymph rig. Both Eric and Tera–Ann Smart were enjoying the benefits the Eagle has to offer as I removed my size 16 Yellow Sally Soft–hackle from fish after fish. Eventually, Tera–Ann snapped off the yellow sally and asked me in her sweet way if I had another "Yellow Soozie." The Yellow Soozie was born, and it has only changed a bit since that day.

The Yellow Soozie also covers a group of flies I like to tie that can represent two different flies. During yellow sally season, we out west usually see pale morning duns (PMDs) hatch concurrently. On days when the hatches occur simultaneously, the Yellow Soozie is incredibly effective because it can mimic both insects at various stages, and this fly provides a subtle "hot–spot" or trigger mechanism. Most of my favorite flies contain some sort of trigger or contrast to "trigger" the fish to eat. The Yellow Soozie triggers fish eats with its red and yellow contrast and soft–hackle movement. Many of these triggers are subtle, maybe a few wraps of pink thread on a mostly black fly, or a wrap or two of tinsel flash on thorax. Some triggers can be much more obvious, using UV finishes and colors. There are also times that my flies will be muted, sparse, and bead–less according to seasons and conditions, and we will discuss these in a later chapter.

Yellow Soozie Hook- Umpqua 2487 #16, Body UTC 70 Hopper Yellow Thread wrapped under Silver Small Wire for rib, Wing- 2 wraps Hungarian Partridge or Light Blue Dyed Hen hackles (shown), Head- Dark Red Uni Thread 6/0- Cement.

Although I don't really focus specifically on the nymph of the sally, I have used variations of a Hare's Ear, Little Yellow Sloans, or Guide's Choice to mimic the sally stonefly. There are more than a few great dry fly patterns for this stonefly, but I prefer Mike Lawson's Henry's Yellow Sally in the appropriate size (usually size 14–16). When fishing the dry, fish it much like you would a caddis, skate it, twitch it, swing it, or dead drift it. A Yellow Stimulator in the right size is also effective. Although I do take advantage of the nymph and adult stage, and the dry fly stage more than the two, I really enjoy drowning the Yellow Soozie under and indicator or in the mini–rig. The old–school Partridge and Yellow is the base for the Soozie, but the few tweaks I've made have enhanced the effectiveness of this fly.

Next in size as we go up the scale is the mysterious skwala. Even the name is mysterious. Like their cousins, they too migrate to the edges to hatch, but I never see their shucks left behind. They are very shy about their emergence and leave virtually no trace that they've made the pilgrimage to hatch. Skwala also come at just the perfect time as water temps are starting to push 45 degrees during the day. It's an end–of–winter treat for fish and I am confident the fish begin to look for them every year at the same time. The nymph is brown to olive brown and can easily be portrayed as a smaller version of a Pat's Rubber Legs. I like to stick to the darker colors with this nymph, because the sun angles are still fairly flat and the darker versions are more inclined to be seen easily and eaten well. I don't often use a dry fly while fishing skwala, but when I do, I've used size 12 Black Foamulators, Black Amy's Ants, and Black Elk Hair Caddis in a size 14.

The beauty of the Skwala is they, like most of their larger cousins, like to hold in clear and quick water with a cobble bottom. Add where they live to their migrating behavior and the fact the water is warming up and trout are beginning to focus on moving water, and you have the perfect storm. What's better than drifting a Skwala through early spring water that forces hungry winter–starved trout to make a quick decision as to whether to eat or not? Not much. As quickly as they show up, they're gone without a trace, like ninjas, I suppose.

Last and not least is the big old golden stone. We have salmon flies in our state, but I rarely get to the waters that provide them, but the nearest stonefly we have to that size and stature is the golden stone. Unlike the skwala, these big bruisers leave nymphal shucks everywhere along the river edge after hatching. They're mocking us, telling us, "You shoulda been here yesterday!" Or are they? Like their cousins, after they hatch they'll be around a while, sometimes up to three weeks, so seeing their signposts is a good thing. You have time.

I will take advantage of the migration that usually begins in July where I frequently fish, but I'm not usually focused on exploiting the nymph of this big stonefly. When I do look to the nymph, I like to tie and fish mine unweighted to get the full benefit of a lively drift over riffles and onto shelves. I like to tie a latex version with soft hackle above the thorax in tan, black, peacock, olive, or a combination thereof. I also enjoy tying the Cracked Stone: either weighted or unweighted, it mimics many characteristics of golden stoneflies. There are many good stonefly nymph patterns out there: just remember to focus on profile and color. I will say this about stonefly nymph patterns: in my opinion, there are only select times to put a yellow stonefly nymph in your rig, and those are during a stonefly molt. When I begin to see shucks float down the river, and the hatch is months away, it tells me the stones are molting. The newly molted nymph is often a bright yellow or creamy color with prominent black dots for eyes. I have had some great days using Kaufmann's Golden Stone in this instance, so there's always a few in my box, just in case.

Cracked Stone Hook–#6-8 MFC 7008, Tail and Legs–Grizzly Barred Rubber legs-Yellow/black or choice, Body-2-3 strands wrapped peacock herl, Thorax-1.0 White Razor foam split and wrapped over Yellow Ice Dub, Wing-Sparse wrapped Partridge, Head-Unweighted thread wrap, or weighted 1/8 Black Countersunk Tungsten bead, Thread-Yellow UTC 170

The arrival of golden stoneflies warms my heart. It means that not only is runoff virtually over and water levels dropping and clarity improving, but I get to really start throwing the mini–rig with conviction. Not that I wasn't using it prior, nor will I quit using it when the goldens are long gone, but it's go time in earnest for the mini–rig. I am going to start fishing runs from the top down, and the golden stone is critical to my success. Now I can start arming my mini–rigs with big "indicator" dries that will float a wet wading boot, are durable, and are easy to see. My go–to golden stonefly dries are the Fuzzy Wuzzy in a size 10 and a Chubby Chernobyl in a size 8–10.

I probably use the Chubby more than the Fuzzy, because it's a bit easier for my clients to see as it bobs on the surface. However, when fishing on my own, I prefer the Fuzzy Wuzzy, because it appears to get more looks and eats. That's not to say the fish don't gobble the Chubby, though: just last year I had a client that hooked and landed a plump 20–inch brown that just slowly elevated to yawn in the big dry, in November. Most years, I use the Chubby, Foamulators, Fuzzy Wuzzies, and Amy's Ants until the water freezes, I like the Chubbys with tan foam bodies, rusty ice dub bodies, white wings for bright sunny days and black foam bodies, and purple or ice–blue dubbed bodies with white wings on overcast and rainy days. As for the others I've mentioned, just match the size profile and color of the insect you're trying to match as you select them.

So, there are my main stones. You can see that I use different stoneflies to my advantage for different ways to catch fish. You may use them completely differently, getting the same or better results. That's the beauty of the sport: there's more than one way to get the job done, according to your geographic area, skill set, and experience. The ten–percenters are always a step ahead of us and may use stoneflies differently, but always customize the usage to you, and don't overlook the obscurities.

MIDGES

Although midges are prolific in the waters I fish, I fish them rarely, probably not as often as I should. Even on our tailwaters in winter, I'll stick to my small BWO nymphs predominately. I think it's just something I've learned from years of guiding: it's hard to keep a client hooked to a fish with a size 22 bug in its mouth. That's not to say I don't fish midges at all. My favorite fly box has a couple of rows of larva, pupa, and adult imposters from size 14 for still waters, up to a size 22 for my favorite rivers.

Midges are like caddis in that they progress from larva to pupa to adult. There are so many different species in this family that I always just refer to the larva as a copper on black, a green on brown, or a red, and then follow that with the size. Pat Dorsey's Black Beauty has become so famous that people think that it's a name of the species within the midge family. Furthermore, Dorsey's Top Secret is becoming the standard out west for the pupa stage of the same bug. Those are two of my favorite midge patterns and you can easily tweak their size, color, flash, or beads to customize them to your water.

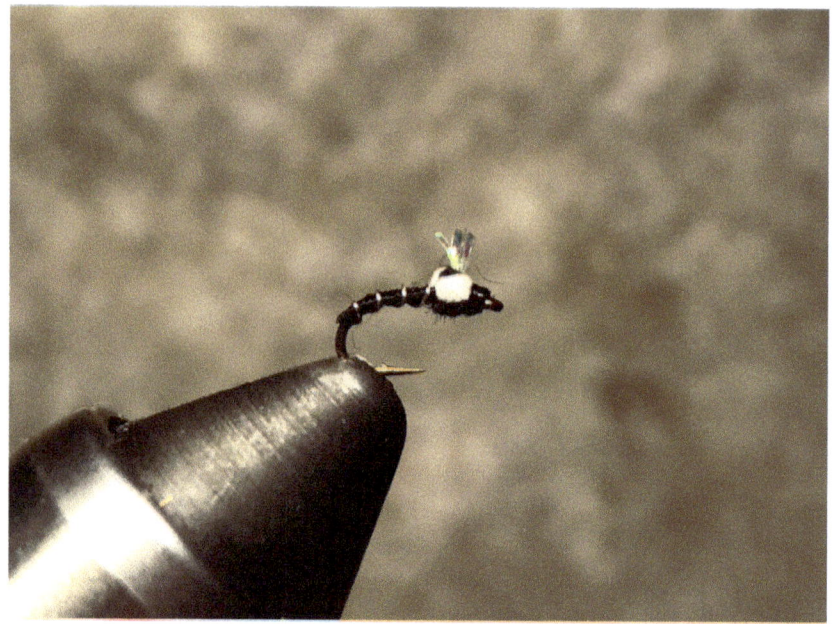

Butt Crack Midge Hook- #18-22 MFC 7125, Body- Black 6/0 Uni Thread with Small Silver Wire wrap, Thorax- White .5 razor Foam Split and pulled over Black Sparkle Dub and 8-10 strands of Pearl Tinsel, Head- Thread wrap

As midges pupate, the thorax becomes large and pronounced and the wing butts become evident. At this point, they generate a bit of gas that creates a bubble that helps them elevate to the surface, where they get captured in the surface film, struggling to make it to adulthood. If you've ever watched mosquitos emerge from a pool of water, then you know exactly what this process looks like. The process I outlined is my favorite stage to fish midges, because they are visible to fish, are lively moving, and get stuck like sitting ducks trying to finish the process. I developed a fly that covers the process quite nicely. It's the Butt Crack Midge. I usually tie it in sizes 18–22. I like copper on black and green on brown, and the silver on black (pictured) best. I will use strands of pearl tinsel to represent the air bubble and wing tips, and the razor foam does a good job providing the bulbous look to pupation. This pattern was also picked up by

Montana Fly Company and is coming to a fly bin near you.

I also enjoy putting the BCM behind a Black Sprout Midge dry fly and allowing it to hang in the surface film. Deadly. I always tie a few patterns with seven or so strands of gray antron matching the length of the body to represent the shuck when I fish the film. Simply tie it in where you'd tie a tail, and it gives the appearance of being stuck in the shuck. Did I say deadly?

The Intangibles

I was talking to a gentleman after a fly fishing show presentation I did in Denver not too long ago. He was telling me how he and a friend were fishing near Wolcott, Colorado on the Eagle during a blinding yellow sally hatch. He was getting fairly animated during our discussion, as he relayed the story of how his friend was whacking fish after fish and he couldn't buy one. As he told the story, he showed me how the yellow sallies were crawling on his face, in his ears and behind his sunglasses. He told me he tried several fly patterns and techniques, including dead drifting yellow sally dries and swinging yellow sally soft hackles to no avail. Finally, he said, he swallowed his pride and yelled to his partner, who had just released another fish, and said, "What the hell are you using?" to which his partner replied, "A size 14 Patriot!"

A Patriot is a gorgeous dry fly tied by a gentleman from Pennsylvania, Charlie Meck. It is one of those flies that works when you least expect it, because it can be used to mimic several different insects, but none well. It's an intangible fly, a ballpark fly, a fly that really doesn't match anything specifically—it is red, white and blue, by the way—but on the other hand, this fly can match the profile of almost everything that floats.

So the gentleman, who has calmed a bit, asked me, "Why was that dang fly working so well?!"

I think he was expecting some long drawn out entomological discussion, and he just stood there looking at me after I said, "It worked so well because it stood out in the crowd."

But then a smile slowly crept across his face. "That's it!" he exclaimed, as he turned and walked away.

Truth is, I don't know why that fly worked so well during that hatch, but I've seen it happen just like that more than once with intangible flies. I'm sure most of you have a few of those in your fly box, either bugs you bought or tied that don't really match a specific insect or food group because of profile or color(s). One of my favorites is the Royal Wolff Coachman. I use this fly a lot on both rivers and still water lakes. It mimics anything from a small BWO to a large callibaetis. One of the best rainbows I've taken from a lake ate the Royal Wolff Coachman after refusing several legitimate callibaetis dries. I could go on with many more examples, but the point is simply this: don't discount the intangible flies, the old stand–by flies, and always have a few handy.

The author with a fine fish taken with a Royal Wulff on the surface.

Streamers

No box is complete without a few streamers. Most often, when guiding, I have to talk clients into using them. I think the reason for this is that most aren't comfortable with the technique. It's not that difficult, and I've covered some basic techniques already. I use streamers anytime I'm on new water and want to get a lay of the land. Like I mentioned, it's a great way to cover a lot of water, looking for fish holds. If I plan on guiding the area in the near future, I'll use the streamers to elicit chases, follows, and bumps, more than hooking fish.

I like variations of white, olive, black, and tan or natural squirrel in my box. John Rohmer's Simi Seal Leech is one of my favorites, as is John Barr's simple and effective Slumpbuster in black. I toss unweighted leeches in with attractors as well, because they are very versatile and easily transition to being drifted under an indicator as well as being fished with streamer techniques. As we discussed last chapter, streamers are incredible fish getters.

Terrestrial, Attractors, and Others

I was talking with my nephew Matt Redford one day, explaining that I really only rely on eight to ten different fly patterns in any given year, which prompted him to ask a very interesting question. He asked, "Do you use them because they catch fish, or do they catch fish because you use them?" I guess the answer is yes, on both accounts. One has to have confidence in the flies one uses, which is a huge part of the equation that is often overlooked. And attractors and terrestrials are part of the program.

Faulkinbury's Hopper Hook-Daiichi 1760 #6 to 10, Wing: Turkey tail with cement, Underwing- red or orange Flourofiber, body; spun and packed Deer Hair, color of choice, Head-Deer Hair bullet head shape, color of choice, Legs-Option 1 round rubber legs, Option 2 Pheasant Tail Legs with hackle wrapped behind bullet head, Tail-Red Deer Hair or red Hackle Fibers.

The imitations in this category have a special place in my fly box, and I rely on their effectiveness. I'm talking about worms, grasshoppers, beetles, ants, scuds, leeches, spiders, and so on. Flies that attract attention and offer up a meal. Folks that fish with me know there's usually a tan San Juan Worm in my nymph rig. If the tan isn't there, then you'll find a pink, black, purple, or red one. Fish like worms. In certain instances, like when I'm fishing a tailwater below a dam, I'll switch out the worm for a scud pattern to match what's coming through the pipes. On the Dream Stream, or Spinney Mountain Ranch near Hartsel, Colorado, my usual attractor is a leech pattern I tie after Landon Mayer's Mini Leech. There's a huge population of leeches in that section: to overlook them as a food group would be ridiculous. Notice how I lump attractors into the equation? I do this because often times, I will use this group of bugs to get the trout's attention more than to solicit an "eat" on the fly. That big leech snaking through the water may not get eaten often, but the BWO emerger below will. Whatever the main attractor food group is, I'm going with it as my attractor. That makes selection simple.

There are also a few attractor terrestrial bugs I like to use in certain situations and certain times of the year. These flies have special uses and should be in every fly box. There's nothing quite as cool as slapping a large hopper pattern a foot off the bank in late September and having a large brown trout hammer it. I like Charlie Craven's Charlie Boy and Faulkinbury's hoppers the most. Their ability to float all day while presenting a fine profile is what makes them shine. I'll often drop a floating beetle behind them, or some sort of dropper below them. Lately, while floating hoppers, I've been dropping twenty-four inches below them to a single, heavily weighted, bead-head Hare's Ear tied on an inverted hook. Bank-slapping ants and beetles the same as hoppers, also has a special place in my heart because it's usually during the fall, and rising fish in September and October is what movies are made of. These flies are also very versatile. If you've never drowned an ant, spider, or beetle under an indicator, you should try it.

WHERE IS THAT DANG FLY?

Nothings worse than getting a butt-kicking on the river, getting an epiphany on what fly to switch to improve your chances, then not being able to find that fly. I'm speaking from experience. I see a lot of guides giving classes on how to organize your fly box these days. Wish I'd thought of that. I think its personal preference when it comes to how you lay out your boxes, but I also think there's a bit of method to the madness.

I am often asked how I organize my fly boxes. I believe how you choose to organize your fly box is not only a personal decision, it is also a task that will evolve with you as an angler. The deeper you get into it, the more your fly boxes begin to fit your fly fishing personality. There are a few basic rules I follow after all these years and dozens of fly boxes I've put together. Let's start with talking about fly box selection.

The make and design of the fly boxes you choose to use is, again, personal. I carry different designs and types at the same time, because of specific needs and traits I am looking for as I spend day after day on the river. I carry two medium-sized waterproof plastic boxes with slit-cut foam. One contains my dry flies sorted by category; the other contains my attractor nymphs and stonefly nymphs. I like these boxes to be waterproof, because they sit low in my waist pack and tend get dunked several times a year, and also because I am in these boxes the least. If I do submerge them, and don't check them in a while, I don't run the risk of the hooks rusting out.

These two boxes have hundreds of flies in many different patterns and colors. In my nymph attractor and stonefly box, on one side I have organized every size and color of Copper Johns, Prince Nymphs, Pheasant Tails, Hare's Ears, and Scuds. The opposite side of this box contains all my Pat's Rubber Legs, Caterpillar patterns, crane fly larva, Cracked Stone flies, Mercers and Kauffman's stones, and damselfly nymphs. These are sorted by size, color, legs or no legs, weighted or non-weighted, and bead or no bead. My fly boxes tend to remind me of my dad's disorganized workbench: it was piled high with tools, but he knew where everything was. My other waterproof box that contains my dry flies also has an extra leaf in the middle and probably contains five hundred surface floating morsels. Not a bad idea to go right now and put your name and phone number on all your boxes if you haven't already.

The dry fly box is separated by category, species, color, size, bug stage, and specialty. I have a section for caddis, mayflies, stoneflies, midges, terrestrial, and specialty/attractor flies. My caddis section has everything from high-viz Elk Hairs to foam post and spent dries, each neatly tucked into a slot in an order that works for me. My mayflies are the same way, organized from drakes to PMDs to Tricos, according to bug stage, color, and size. I have a couple of rows dedicated to yellow sally stoneflies of various design, large Stimulators, and a row of large golden stone representations. As for the midges, I employ a lot of Sprout Midge dries, Irresistibles, Griffith's Gnats, and other basic midge cluster patterns. I've a dedicated section for small grasshopper patterns, foam beetles of various colors, and several ant patterns. The last category, the specialty bugs, includes a few fly patterns that are special and nostalgic to me, and they catch fish. I am referring to size fourteen to sixteen Royal Wulffs, Deer Hair Adams, Hair Wing Peacock Ladies, and Patriots. These flies continue to catch fish for me when others fail, and take me back to my childhood. It's important to note that every species of fly I carry in the dry fly box is covered with a dun, spent, drowned, emerger, pupa, spinner, CDC, stuck-in-the-shuck, and crippled stages somewhere in my other boxes.

The next box to discuss contains all my soft-hackled representations. This box is divided by size, color, species, and whether they are beaded. This is where I carry dozens of black, tan, natural, yellow, or orange soft hackles in sizes fourteen to twenty. This box is on top of the last two we talked about because I'm in this box many times daily. It also contains a few specialty bugs, including spiders, winged wets, Barr's Graphic Caddis, Kingrey's Ice Caddis, and Crazy Ladies. Basically, anything I need that can be dead drifted, lifted, or swung goes into this box.

My last box is my go-to box and contains caddis and midge larva, Bluewinged Olive, Trico, and PMD nymphs and emergers; and my indicator dry flies for the mini-rig. This is an all foam box with eleven raised foam sections on one side and flat foam on the other. To give you an idea of the scope of this box, the flat foam side, at this moment, contains forty-nine indicator bugs ranging from Fuzzy Wuzzies, Chubby Chernobyls, Amy's Ants, Faulkinbury's Deer Spun Hoppers, and size twelve and up Craven's Charlie Boy Hoppers. Again, all are organized by size and color. The opposite side of this box is fairly simple and contains flies no larger than a size sixteen. These are my base flies, sorted by stage, species, and color. From bottom to top, you'll find organized midge and caddis larvae and accompanying pupae. The midges include the Butt Crack Midge in red, brown, and black; my Black Mamba Midge pupae; Garcia's Rojo Midges; and Dorsey's Top Secret. The caddis are simple patterns of larva in rust, cream, yellow, chartreuse, and brown and are all unweighted.

Next in this box, you'll find the rows dedicated to Pheasant Tails, Butt Crack PMDs, Barr's Emergers, Craven's Two Bit Hookers, BCBs in purple and brown, Solitude's RSII with flash thorax added (nicknamed Chocolate Thunder), Chung's RSII in gray and black, and various patterns crippled and drowned in each species of mayfly I have the pleasure to use. I also carry a plastic puck containing all my San Juan representations, in tan, pink, red, cream, and purple, and a few attractor eggs in "cheese", amber, green, and "clown" colors. It's my proverbial "can o' worms" and I don't get near the river without it. I also carry a puck containing leeches, Barr's Slumpbusters, leech patterns, and various weighed and unweighted streamer patterns I tie using John Rohmer's Simi Seal.

My go-to box's contents ebb and flow as the seasons and water conditions change during the year. At times, you'd be hard pressed to find more than a few PMD patterns, as other bugs are more prolific according to what the fish and season is telling me. Mysteriously, as the seasons change, my favorite patterns begin to multiply and push other less useful bugs out. That doesn't mean I don't have several of those flies ready to go; they just vacate my go-to box and reside in a large auxiliary box I carry in my truck just in case.

I carry four fly boxes and three pucks of flies at all times when guiding or fishing on my own. Pucks are those clear plastic fly boxes, about the size of a hockey puck, with a lid included. As for the box you choose, again, that's personal, but I like different types for different classes of bugs. For example, I like my dry fly (including attractors) and heavily weighted bug (including stones, scuds, etc.) boxes to have the additional sleeve in the middle and to be completely waterproof when closed and locked. Again, I can carry many patterns and don't have to worry about them getting wet and rusting because I only go into those boxes at certain times of the year. The other two boxes I carry are two–sided and have foam exteriors. I get into these boxes a lot, and if I drop them, they'll float long enough for me to grab them. Believe me, I've chased them downriver like many of you before!

I began this chapter talking about the two guys picking out flies for the day, and explaining that it's not guesswork that helps you in fly selection, but historical, seasonal, and conditional data combined with experience. When you get to this point in your career, people think you are clairvoyant, because you are able to predict, with some form of certainty, what may happen that day as far as flies and hatches are concerned. If you miss your prediction, you will have a back–up plan in place, because you are always striving to stay in front of the hatch, not only conditionally, but seasonally as well. Mama Nature always wins, but it's always fun to play along, and try to match wits with her. It's not guesswork if you have a strong foundational knowledge of insect behavior, are willing to look for the obscurities, have a blue–collar idea of entomology, and take advantage of this information each time out. Now where's that bin with leggy–flies?

You're Soaking in It

A COUPLE OF years ago, during an out-of-state fly fishing presentation I was giving, an audience member asked me if I was a float or wade guide. I told him that I only wade guided, to which he began clapping. I wasn't sure why he was clapping, but I ran with it, explaining that I liked the ability to really pick runs apart piece by piece. Sure, you'll get to point B if you float with me, but your casts will go from six to sixty feet in a blink of an eye, and you better be wearing a floatation device.

Point is, wading fits my style (and skill set). It allows me to literally get into the water, feel it and my surroundings, and dial in as best I can to the present situations. We've discussed much to this point, and now that your feet are wet, you have the opportunity to go from average to elite. Now is the time to think like an elite angler, the ten-percenter, that angler who always seems to be landing a fish. This is the chapter that I was referring to when I said, "We will discuss this in detail later." This is it. Let's dig in.

For a minute, let's review what in my mind constitutes a mile-marker-five fly angler. This person can present (cast) close to where he or she is looking for moderate distances of up to thirty feet, knows when to mend upstream or downstream, can set, can fight fish while landing 30 percent or so, can pull good fly representations out of the box, and can tie on his or her own bugs. This person can also read the water horizontally, and has the concept of reading the water vertically. Let's talk about some obscurities to get this person to the next level.

Short-and Long-Line Mending

I always tell folks that you can't play if you can't mend. Short–line mending is fairly straightforward and simple: mending gets more difficult the more line you have out. One rule of thumb even the elite use is if you feel as if you're doing more mending than drifting, you have hit your skill–imposed mending limit. In other words, if you feel like you can't keep up the mending process, you have too much line out. There are situations where I think, *Holy smokes, I can't keep up with this drift. I need to change positions, shorten up, and get back in my wheelhouse.* I don't care who you are: you simply can't set the hook quickly enough on most nymphing drifts where you can't control the drift. At least not on the trout where I live: they spit too quickly. I want the ability to mend with fifty feet of line out as a skill set. I don't like my chances if I have to try to set with a bunch of line out past my mending and drifting skill set. Over–exuberant lengths cause too many missed fish and foul hook–ups. I hesitate to assign specified lengths to folks regarding their skill sets, so let's just say if you have to work too hard to mend and keep up with the mending, it's a good idea to shorten up to where you're comfortable.

Another common problem with overextending your drift cast length is that it forces the angler to fish with a fly rod angle that is well above parallel to the river surface. You are forced to hold the fly rod to a high angle to get as much line off the water as possible. With all that line out on the water, you become extremely slow on the set, and when you do set, because of the poor rod angle, you don't have enough rod left to actually straighten out the line to firmly set the hook. I like a fly rod that is nearly parallel to the water when drifting under my fly rod tip out to about twenty feet, and a fly rod that doesn't break a fifteen–degree upward angle on longer drifts. Let me be very clear here. I am not talking about fly rod height off the water, such as chest–high, shoulder–high, or head–high. I am strictly talking about the fly rod angle at various heights over the water.

I know some of you are saying, "But wait, it's okay if I put a more aggressive up–ward angle to my fly rod when I nymph. I do it all the time, and I catch fish." Then ask yourself this question: why don't you do it when you're fishing dry flies, dry drops, or streamers? Could you imagine fishing Tenkara–style with a highly angled fly rod? How about Czech–style nymphing or any other tight–line discipline? The point is, folks think they can get away with anything as long as they have mended to the indicator. The indicator becomes a crutch, but it's not the most important part of an indicator nymph rig: the flies still are.

Unlike Tenkara and some of the European nymphing skills, we rely on the indicator because we are not *directly* connected to the flies. There's a hinge in between, actually two in an in–line nymph rig. Those styles allow for more diverse rod angles during the drift because there is a direct connection which allows for quicker reaction on the set, and more control throughout the drift. Don't get me wrong, I enjoy nymphing under an indicator, but the indicator does nothing more than tell you what's already happened. It's like the old remote controls for older televisions; there was a discernable pause from the time you made your selection to the time the television reacted. For these reasons, elite fishers nymph with proper fly rod angles, and stay within their self–imposed skills. The best nymph fly fishers I know catch fish right under their rod tip, out to thirty to thirty–five feet consistently and comfortably. You have to start somewhere, so you might as well focus in close and perfect the drift mechanics.

Bob Streb showing proper rod, hand and body positioning as he short line nymph drifts with a ten foot fly rod. Notice the size of the management loop, elite anglers can fish with larger than average loops.

The short–line mend is quick and simple to master. With a nice, flat fly rod, mid–chest level or higher, you simply lift the line off the water and place it either upstream, downstream, or a combination of both, to remove all the drag imparted from the fly line. You can only mend what you can take off the water, and this "up–and–over" action with the fly rod is simple to master with an amount of line no more than the length of your fly rod from the rod tip. Don't confuse short–line mending and drifts with tight–line drifts. Tight–line fishing is a different technique, and we don't want a tight line, meaning no slack in the line, when we are working with an indicator or surface flies. The obscurity, or what the ten–percenters know, is with too little or zero slack in the short–line nymph drift or dry fly drift, the drift becomes rigid and doesn't follow the horizontal or vertical grids naturally.

There is a fine line between too little and too much slack, but if you're going to err, err on the side of a bit too much. Still, try to keep those instances few and short-lived. If your fly line is too tight to the indicator, keeping the indicator in the seam you placed it in is nearly impossible. The river seam where you place your indicator or dry fly upon casting will rarely move downstream in a perfectly straight line. Even when short-lining, you will want to place your initial mend all the way to the indicator or dry fly while usually mending in slack, quickly picking up as much line as necessary in the management loop, while all the while looking for forming hinges. This is why a high, flat fly rod is so incredibly helpful: you will be able to make all the adjustments you need quickly, without ever taking your eyes off the indicator or dry fly.

The author demonstrating drifting the flies in the same plane as the indicator. Also notice the amount of slack in the drift, the rod position and how the hands are in position to work together to retain focus on the indicator.

Not only will you not lose focus on the business end of the fly line, you will be in perfect position to set anytime during the drift. I observe this characteristic when watching the elite. They are never out of position, are never behind in a mend, completely control the management loop, and are in perfect position to set on any/

every drift. Additionally, because the river rarely flows in a straight line, the added slack will allow you to keep the dry fly or indicator in the horizontal plane you put it in initially. For example, if you are fishing a seam and it gently flows away from your position, added slack is necessary to keep flies in the same plane you initially put them in. If there is not enough slack in this instance, the flies will begin to be pulled out of the seam toward the angler. This is very often imperceptible to the inexperienced angler, and will most definitely destroy your drift. When folks book a day fishing with me because they want to get to the next level, one of the first things I diagnose is whether they are drifting in the same plane throughout the drift. It's observable.

As you can see, even short–line mending has a lot of moving parts. This is why I'm so adamant about not out–casting your ability to mend. I see it all the time with mile–marker–five or –six anglers. They have just enough skill casting to ruin their ability to mend and catch fish. Here's a scenario I see every now and then. An angler comes fishing with me that fits the description above. I talk briefly with them and ask that they begin by working a seam about ten feet off their rod tip. I further explain how I intend to work this run in grid line increments, how we are going to focus on mending and line management, and how we are going to really dial in depth and speed. I get a couple of steps into going to work with the angler's partner, and they are shooting thirty–five–foot casts over several beautiful holds, effectively spooking every feeding fish in there. The partner usually really follows instructions after seeing this, and out fishes their buddy five to one for the day.

Long–line mending is a skill you develop over time, and with plenty of practice with short–line techniques. Folks ask me plenty what a well–mended drift looks like. I can tell you more easily what it doesn't look like. It doesn't look like the indicator or surface flies are being pushed or pulled in any direction by the fly line on the water. It also doesn't look like there is too little slack as to pull the indicator around the angler. It doesn't appear to have too much fly line on the water. It doesn't seem that there is no control because of an inordinate amount of fly line in the water by the anglers' feet. So it looks tidy and clean for full, quick sets, with a bit of slack as a shock absorber for various seams. The management loop is usually not over eight feet (four feet to a side), and is always being sucked in or pulled out, depending on what the angler needs.

In a long–line mend, a mend that is a couple of times the length of your fly rod and better, typically your first mend is the most critical. If you short–arm this one and don't get a complete mend all the way to the indicator or surface flies, you'll be playing catch–up for the rest of the drift. If this happens to you consistently, it's a pretty good sign you need to back off the length of your casts. Long–line mends put plenty of line on the water. Between your fly rod tip and end of your fly line may be dozens of seams with differing speeds. Each one can provide the need for a mend. Your fly line may have several larger mend corrections, a few smaller corrections, and a combination of upstream and downstream mends for every drift.

The fact there is so much going on in long–line mending is why elite anglers strive to stay as short as possible with casts, to allow for exemplary, perfectly mended drifts. Thinking over my fly fishing career, I can think of only a few times where I had to give up completely on a run I couldn't effectively drift, because I couldn't effectively mend the length I needed. I either moved closer or found a way to the other side of the river. It has always made more sense to me to try to get closer than to beat the water up, spook the fish, and miss the set if I should entice an eat. If most anglers can't reach it, an elite angler with more skills will have a shot at some pretty good water.

Hinges

Hinges are constantly forming anytime you put a fly line in the water. Even when you're tossing streamers, it's there. You just don't focus on it much because you don't usually see it, and it's not a drift–killer when throwing streamers. Mile–marker–six folks begin to understand hinges and their debilitating effects on drifts that require the fly line to surface float. Hinges can form anytime you have differing speeds on the water's surface, or seams. Large hinges are easily recognized: it's the subtle ones that get you. Hinges cause drag. Drag forces your flies out of intended seams and destroys drift speed control.

John Barr created the Copper John, a nifty fly that is still very effective today. The Copper John is a heavier fly comprised of a weighted head and several wraps of wire. It was all the rage, and rightly so, for years. I think this was because the Copper John accounted for hinges in the drift. The added weight, which comes built into the fly, helped slow down the nymph drift in spite of the hinges, allowing lower skilled anglers good enough drifts to catch more fish. Although it allows for many more fish in the net, the fact that the angler is not having to mend to subtle hinges defeats the purpose. This goes for all weighted flies: they mask a lot of errors people make in the indicator nymph drift. Try fishing unweighted flies and identify the hinges. Then you can develop the ability to slack, feather, and micro–mend to hinges. Once you dial in this skill, you are on your way to the next level. This obscure skill, once you master it, will put you to the next mile marker quickly.

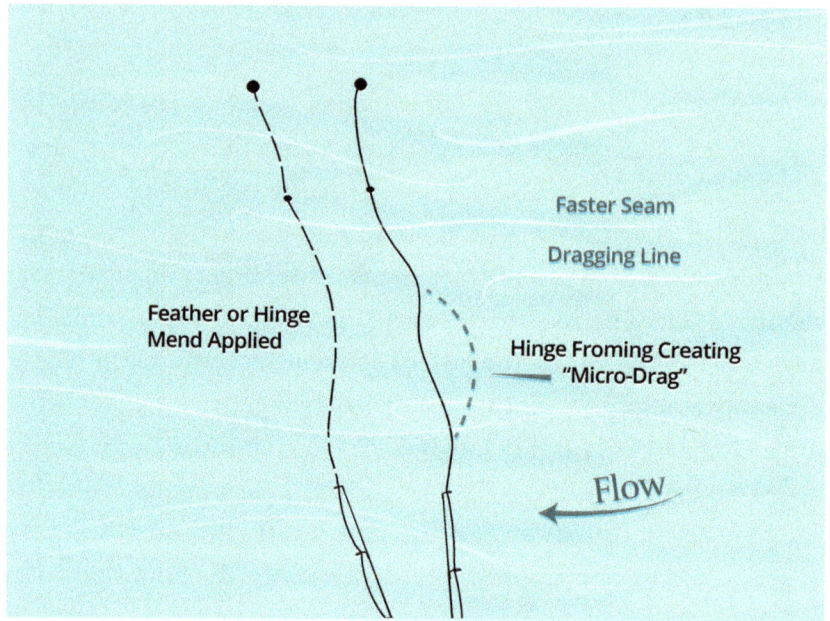

Hinge and Correction

Hinges can appear in your line anywhere from your rod tip to the end of your fly line during the drift. They can even form in your leader. The slower the water, the subtler they are, because they form very slowly and are almost imperceptible. What you're looking for is a section of line, any length, which is dragging or causing drag to its adjacent section. Looking at the diagram, you can see a small adjustment is needed to remove the drag from the hinge presented. I call mending a hinge a micro or feather mend. Most often, depending on how far the hinge is from the end of the fly rod tip, the mend is a subtle as the hinge. It only takes a small movement to mend the hinge in the opposite direction from which it's being pulled or pushed. Often times, it also requires a small amount of slack thrown in. You may be required to throw feather mends anywhere along your line in the drift, from near to far, one after the next, to achieve a truly drag–free drift with unweighted flies.

More Digging

Let's dig into the dry fly and then the dry dropper drifts. Like most all fly fishers, I really enjoy those days when there's a solid hatch and the fish are feeding on the surface. It's a fun challenge to sneak through the river, setting up on surface feeding trout. In most cases, your casts have to be considerably longer than with your standard indicator rig, because added distance from your quarry helps prevent spooking fish with fly rod flash or other movement. When fishing an indicator rig, you can get by with one movement roll casting because the fish are typically sub–surface, well below the water level. Throwing dry flies usually requires much more movement in a full–cast mode. The elite dry fly fishers know this and know another important detail that prevents many anglers from getting to the next level. Whereas a nymph drift is most often a short cast with a long drift, a dry fly cast is most often a long cast with a short drift.

Elite dry fly fishers have the mechanics, cast distances, and angles figured out. They also know where to cast to surface feeding fish because of where the fish *will* be, not because of where the fish took the adult insect. There are three types of riseforms of fish feeding on the surface.

In a surface eat, the mouth breaks the water. Look for a big bubble that can be formed as a fish breaks the surface, mouth open. Often such a bubble appears, offering a clue to how it's feeding. The next thing you're looking for is where the fish was originally staged before it rose to eat. Did it rise and follow the fly a short distance without breaking perpendicular? That was a compound rise. Did it rise and follow the fly while breaking perpendicular, to eat it going away? That's a complex rise. The fish follows the insect in both those rises, then returns to its original position. Do you see the issue? If we cast to where we saw the fish take the insect, in both cases we would be casting directly on top of or downstream of the target. Therefore, you must always discern what riseform a fish is creating as it feeds on top. We will discuss the simple riseform later in this chapter.

Dry fly fishing doesn't only require longer, finer leaders (I like a 9' 5x with 6x tippet), longer casts, and exemplary mending techniques: it requires a shift in thinking. The only way to shift this thinking is to incorporate the rhythm of the river and cadence of feeding fish. Sounds goofy, I know, but the ten–percenters know this and perfect the ability to drop down a couple of gears and slowly work the water piece by piece. Gone is your typical forty–five–degree upstream to sixty–degree downstream drift. Now you should be focusing on a single target fish or small target area and your casts can be at any angle and any length.

The Eagle River offers some exemplary dry fly action during the year. I see it often. Setting up on a surface feeding fish, armed with a double–dry rig in my client's hands, I'll say, "Okay, nice and easy, four feet upstream of the last rise. Lay it up in there with a little slack. Don't mend: we don't want to spook her." What happens here more often than not to inexperienced dry fly fishers is that they instinctively throw a cast way upstream at a forty–five–degree angle. In other words, they go back to the nymph drift presentation. It still comes down to two things: the fly fishing formula, and letting the fish see only the flies—no fly line, no fly rod flash. It comes down to speed and depth of flies, which is negligible when fishing dry flies to feeding fish. Provided you are keeping your drifts short, well–mended, and in the same plane as the feeding fish, you throw in a dry fly that is close to what the fish are feeding on without a bunch of line–slap, and you've got it.

I was fishing with John Frey one day not too long ago. John is a longtime client that has turned into a good friend. We have great fly fishing adventures together. One day, we were fishing the Eagle River near the town of Wolcott, when we found ourselves in the middle of a black caddis hatch. The fish began to pop the surface everywhere in the glide in which we were standing, and we began to move several fish on a two-bug dry rig consisting of a yellow sally dry and a size eighteen Black Elk Hair Caddis. We stuck to the formula, using only necessary, long quartering upstream or direct upstream casts, short drifts, and a heavy dose of stealth. By chance, I glanced upstream and spied a large dorsal fin protruding from the water that just so happened to be connected to a twenty-inch rainbow. I pointed her out to John.

Now being an experienced, elite angler, John didn't go directly into a cast toward this fish. We stood and watched for a bit, snipped down to a single fly as we left the caddis attached, while devising a plan, and getting her feeding cadence. The rainbow was about forty feet upstream of us, to our left as we looked upstream, about ten inches off the bank in about eight inches of water. To compound the difficulty, she was tucked behind a small bush that protruded into the water off the bank about a foot and a half above her.

"Got her right where we want her, Johnny," I whispered, to which he replied, "Let's get this beast."

We chuckled as I motioned us a little closer. It's not that John can't make that sort of cast, but I failed to mention we also were enjoying intermittent gusts of wind, up to twenty-five miles an hour from left to right. I told John to wait for a wind lull, and to shoot for a spot three to four feet above the fish. "Make sure you leave some slack, so we don't have to mend and possibly spook her, and for heaven's sake, keep the line off the top of her ," I demanded.

John glanced over his left shoulder and down at me, and asked, "Is that all?"

"Yep," I said, then we both smiled as he went into a back cast.

There comes a time, when you watch the elite doing anything in motion, that you just shake your head and smile. There was no luck involved as John made that cast and drift in one shot. We landed that fish, and I think John would tell you himself that he couldn't have pulled that off even a couple of years prior. His technique, experience, and knowledge have collided to make him an accomplished angler.

John Frey with a nice winter Cutthroat from the South Platte River near Hartsel, Colorado. Experienced anglers have a calm confidence about them.

Keep Digging: The Mini-Rig

The double dry, or dry fly single dropper, can be fished virtually the same. With a single dropper, I can run a film fly a couple of inches below the surface, or drop the fly effectively a couple of feet below the dry. Sticking to the formula to ensure a collision with the fish, and with casts in any direction, but predominately quarter-to-hard upstream, with as little mending as you can get away with for a short drift is, in my opinion, the most effective method for dry and dry-dropper fishing. When it comes to the mini-rig, well that's a different story.

It's called a mini-rig because it's basically a mini-nymph rig, but because of the indicator being replaced with a nice big dry fly, we don't necessarily have to be too concerned with casting in close proximity to surface feeding fish and spooking them. Now, any cast can and will spook fish if it slaps or fish see the fly line, so you have to avoid that, but by and large, a big dry fly is much less obtrusive than an indicator. The mini–rig drift can also take on the look of a long nymph drift, so it performs well in short and long drifts respectively. However, like any drift, the better the drift is set up before entering the target area, the better chance you have of a good drift through the target area. It you're blind dry dropping to likely water, attempt to make nice, long, quality drifts. If you're working a smaller section, work for perfect short drifts over the likely holding water. As always, anticipate the next mend.

I mentioned my rule before, but it bears repeating. For every fish I see feeding on the surface, there are three more feeding just below it. I enjoy dry fly fishing, but really enjoy catching or having clients catch as many fish as possible. The mini–rig usually takes precedence over the dry fly rig, and produces plenty of action from riffles to tailouts, but this and many other rigs are absolutely useless when one scenario rears its ugly head.

Every person that fishes a bunch has heard of the dog days of fly fishing. Depending on your location, it usually starts in late July or August and goes until the autumn caddis and pseudo Baetis begin to come off in mid–September. Water temperatures are rising while flows are falling, and the sun is high overhead, permeating the water. Between those conditions and a lot of angling pressure on the rivers, well, it just gets tougher. What I begin to see—and my data reinforces this—is that the fish from one body of water to the next begin to suspend in the middle columns. They aren't inclined to eat dries on top or nymphs on the bottom regularly, but they are feeding, most times feeding heavily, usually amongst large obstructions for safety.

If you watch them, they will elevate up to a full body length to eat an emerger of some sort, then freight–train straight back down to the original holding position. I have watched them do this for hours. Many of you are probably thinking that there is a simple rig for this: your standard dry dropper. Simply determine the fish's depth, tie on the sinking appropriate dropper to match the depth at or slightly above the feeding fish, and hocus pocus, fish on, right? Wrong, in this case. Fact is, at this time of the year the fish are focused on one stage of one bug and one feeding behavior. It happens other times of the year as well, in other scenarios, but it's not so dang obvious as in this one: these fish are blatantly giving you the middle fin. When feeding like this, these fish are not at all interested in your emerger pattern floating drag–free straight down main street at one consistent level. Nope, they are keyed into emergence, real emergence. These fish want to have the flies lifted in front of them at the proper speeds and hatch emergence angles according to water speeds. Yup, this is an obscure method, and is deadly if done properly.

Mandy Hertzfeld demonstrating proper lift mechanics as she lifts the flies in front of an obstruction.

It's not unusual to be in the fly shop this time of year, listening to guides and folks off the street lament that the dang fish just aren't cooperating. "We're dry–dropping stuff right on their beaks, but they still aren't eating!" I hear it all the time during the dog days. I beat my head against several submerged rocks for years, trying to figure out how to get these fish to consistently eat my offerings. I came up with a technique that works for me, and it's an emergence lift. This is not unlike a normal lift technique, which is great for lifting in front of rocks or other obstructions, but this emergence lift takes things one step further.

Let's first talk about the normal lift technique so we can establish common ground. I use the lift all the time when fly fishing. It's usually associated with nymphing, but can be used to bring any subsurface offering up through the columns to feeding fish. It's a simple motion. Lift your fly rod at the appropriate speeds and angles to pull the flies up through the water columns. It's really effective in front of obstructions, but you can use it anywhere within the drift. It elicits several responses from fish. First off, if done properly, it looks like emergence;. that'll give you many strikes. Second, it spurs the greed or competition gene in fish. They have to eat it before the other fish, or simply before it gets away, out of greed. This technique, although similar to the emergence lift, is also different. Let's dig deeper.

First off, I take all beads of all flies after the Fourth of July. Bears repeating, "No bead–fly after the Fourth of July." Next, I run a minimum of nine–foot leaders, but still run 4x fluorocarbon tippets. I don't have a need to run the lower sighter in this case, because I will feel the fish eat, and I like to take it off just to make sure I'm not spooking fish as I lift the entire rig in front of them. Leave the upper section of sighter in place: it helps you determine when the indicator turns over, and gives you a good look at exactly where your upper leader section is in relation to the indicator at all times.

You need heavier, somewhat invisible tippets, because of the way these fish are eating. You see, these fish are predominately hooked as they move back down to their original suspended spot right after eating on the lift. As you can imagine, as you lift, they are moving down, thus the term "freight–training." When they realize they're hooked, they continue toward the bottom like they're on fire, just as you realize you have a fish on and sometimes can react too hard in an upward angle. You can see the need for heavier tippets.

I am going to use either a small plastic bobber or a yarn and rubber band indicator for this method. There will be at least five feet from indicator to weight in the in–line, two–or–three–bug nymph rig. The water depth at which I usually see this fish feeding behavior is about four to six feet, a slower glide section, and out for all to see. The fish usually are set up in the middle or upper middle column and never come within a foot of breaking the surface. My real concern with setting the depth is I want to make sure the flies are below the feeding fish by at least eighteen inches, and are *at that depth* at least four feet upstream of the fish depending on water speeds. This is where the upper sighter helps, but again, you're going to have to experiment! The idea is to mimic an emerging insect as it rises through the columns *and* drifts downstream. How long does this emergence take? It takes about as long as it takes to eat a handful of popcorn. In other words, results may vary. You have to keep experimenting with it, but once you dial it in, it's an amazingly effective and fun way to fish. Err on the side of lifting too slowly at first, as you practice this maneuver.

Find the fish feeding this way on emergers, identify the fly they are eating by looking at the naturals hatching, get the size and color close, get the weight dialed in along with the depth, line the fish up with your belly button or in the middle of the drift if possible, and use the formula to calculate how far upstream you have to present and when you should start the lift. Present the flies, mend appropriately and with plenty of slack to allow for full sink, and maintain a good fly rod angle. If you've done things properly to this point, you begin your lift when the indicator is a couple of feet upstream of your target fish and in the same seam. Slowly lift up and slightly over your downstream shoulder, all the while pulling in line with your management loop. The faster the water speeds, the sooner you begin to lift; the slower, the later. Really, it boils down to this: how well can you mimic a true emergence with a fly rod? The neat thing is, you'll be able to see the fish react, so there's no need to try to look for your flies subsurface. Simply change your drift depths, speeds, and lifts according to how the fish react.

The method I just described is great for fish that are within a fly rod's length of your rod tip. Where this gets a bit more interesting and infinitely harder to describe is when the fish are in the twenty-to-thirty-foot range in front of you and you can't squeeze closer. This emergence lift technique is obscure enough; now we're throwing in another variable. Not going to lie: this is a difficult technique now, but incredibly rewarding. Okay, here goes. Align the feeding fish into the lower one third of the nymph drift. For discussion's sake, put them at the ¾ mark of your nymph drift. You will need to add distance and a bit of extra weight to your rig for depth and speed allowance. Now, try to cast as far upstream as possible into the seam your target fish are in downstream. Immediately, cleanly mend or cast much additional slack, maybe up to fifteen feet worth of line mended into the drift. Add or subtract line as you mend and drift until you get to about the center point of your drift. Let your brain calculate according to water speeds, depth, and fly location when to lift. Use the upper sighter section to help out on fly location. Okay, the lift is going to be easier to do than to explain.

As your indicator gets to mid-drift, throw a hard slack mend upstream, then drop the level of the fly rod while keeping it flat to the water, as you suck in line with the management loop. Your brain will supply the timing, but you now need to begin the lift by raising the level of the fly rod, eventually letting it break the fifteen-degree upward angle barrier as you raise your arm over your head and lean downstream. This move is fairly difficult, and I find it easier without an indicator because of drift mechanics and behaviors with an indicator. The hard part is lifting while keeping it in the proper seam. It's especially tough if the seam is moving away from you, but very doable if the seam is moving toward you as it flows. I have taught many this technique and it works, especially since fish don't see this technique every day and they are laser-focused on their feeding behavior. The biggest mistakes anglers make when attempting this technique are not allowing the flies to be all the way down to the substrate before the lift, and "cross–lifting," bringing the flies up through two different seams during one lift. Again, experiment.

Skinny Rig

I've already spilled the beans on the long and lean nymph rig designed for shallow clear water and spooky fish nymphing. Let's take a minute to talk about the skinny rig. I've been using this for many years, and its effectiveness continues to amaze me. It's pretty obscure, and catches many fish when dry flies aren't working as well as one might want during a hatch, especially when the fish are dialed into one stage of one bug, in one slot, while feeding one way.

The skinny rig is effective year–round. I've used it from midge to BWO, from Trico spinner falls to caddis hatches, although it shines brightest during a BWO or PMD hatch out west. I am confident it will work anywhere there's emerging insects and trout. One just needs to dial in size, stage, and color of the naturals to pull this off. I am looking for two specific trout riseforms. You can certainly catch many fish this way with only one riseform, but if I can get a combination of trout sipping on duns with a simple rise, and trout eating emergers just below the film, this rig is downright filthy.

A simple rise is where the trout maintains one feeding station, moves up to feed while sliding slightly upstream, breaks the surface with an open mouth, eats, and then slides back into roughly the same feeding slot and depth. This feeding pattern is what I'm looking for. The compound and complex rising fish can fall to this technique too, but it's more difficult because of the factors outlined previously. When you find trout feeding in this way, in any type of water, it's time to go skinny. I'm always barking about how versatile the in–line nymph rig can be. This is a great example of what I'm talking about.

This rig is one reason I like monofilament leaders when I nymph fish. I can easily convert the nymph rig into the skinny rig without having to worry about extra leader sink I would encounter using fluorocarbon. Take off or adjust the indicator to at least five feet from the weight. Now remove that weight. At this point you have a few decisions to make regarding fly choices. Usually, I have been nymphing with my clients, throwing an attractor (probably a San Juan Worm), a soft hackle as a middle bug, and a BCB emerger to match the hatch as my point fly. Remember, through data and experience, I should already have the proper flies. Most often, I will dry the San Juan Worm, and apply some silicon floatant to it and the tippet. Now here is where you have to be careful. Don't go back to the typical nymph drift! Apply the fly fishing formula. Pick out a single feeding fish and get its feeding cadence, and present a cast upstream that will put the well–mended flies right at the fish's level. Set on the "swirl" of the fish feeding, or if you scooted up the indicator and left it on, set on the indicator pause. The set here is much like a dry fly set, an up–and–over lift on the downstream shoulder. Be easy here. Remember, you've been nymphing for a time, and the tendency is to over–set and snap–off.

During a spinner fall after mating, I will remove the San Juan Worm, and replace it with a fly that can represent a spent or crippled version of the bug that's falling spent at the end of a hatch. It's not that the San Juan Worm is causing issues. On the contrary, you'd be amazed at how many fish eat the worm skinny. I just like to go "spent" with that top fly to hedge my bets. Be very careful when you first use this technique. Again, folks will snap off the first time doing this, because of the fact they've been using an aggressive nymph set before going skinny. Set firmly, and give the fish plenty of room to run. They get a little pissed when you fool them this way.

When you're soaking in the river, it's time to be precise with your actions, have a reason for what you're doing and where you're doing it, and have the confidence to experiment and use less than obvious techniques. Sure, there's a systematic, foundational component to this sport if you want to be successful, but there's also a think–big, take–risks component that, if inserted properly into your program, will pay huge dividends. If you want to get better fast, learn the foundation well and then think outside the box. Heck, throw the box away.

Wanna Get Better Fast?

I AM OFTEN asked after giving a fly fishing presentation, "How do I get better fast?" Although there's no substitute for many hours of quality time on the river, I do believe there's a way to improve your skills quickly, efficiently locate the holes in your fly fishing game, and promptly brush up on your fly fishing skills. Go fish the small stuff. Fly fish the small rivers out West or the creeks in the Midwest, Southern, or Eastern parts of the country. I'm referring to "highway" water, water that is as wide as a two–lane highway. These are small bodies of moving water that have many different characteristics, such as tight quarters, overhanging canopy, brush filled edges, many bends and straights, and quick water that transitions from one part of the run to another in less time than it takes to read the last sentence.

Some folks raise an eyebrow when I mention this, but when I begin to reason why, I usually see heads nod in affirmation. Small water, no matter what species of fish you're chasing, forces you to put all your skills to the test. Everything you do has to be well thought out, you must be clean and precise, and you must anticipate not only the next mend and cast, but where and how you going to finish the job when you hook a fish. Small water will bring out the best and worst in an angler.

When you read the surface of small water, you have to really concentrate, because it transitions so quickly, locating certain parts of a run can be difficult. Combine this with what can be incredibly short runs, and you have to think quickly on your feet. The vertical grid is much more compressed, but still exists. The horizontal grid must go bank to bank because you need to cover all the water, every inch. Reading the grids is easy compared with how you may have to set up just to make a presentation and drift. This simple fact will draw on all your skills, and provides a great way to improve quickly.

Flinging the Small Stuff

Even though you are probably able to easily roll cast across the small water, precision and the ability to perform a few specialty casts is paramount. This isn't about overpowering the fly rod or having a large margin for error, this is about direction and distance control. Even a simple roll cast must be calculated and measured, movement must be kept to an absolute minimum, and presentations must be light and peaceful. Small water forces you to be able to perform every cast, from a water–loaded upstream roll cast to a precise tuck cast off your knees on the first attempt.

Gentry Smith showing stealth while working to a surface feeder on a small Arizona high country stream. Photo courtesy Michael Faulkinbury

If you're inclined, dropping down in fly rod length and weight is not a bad idea. A seven–and–a–half–foot, three–weight rod is a blast to throw on small water along with smaller–diameter leaders and tippets. My favorite rod to use is on the small stuff is an eight–foot, four–weight, Cherry Series from 8 Rivers Fly Rods. Compact, quick, and presents delicately. For practice, I like to stick with my usual rod sizes and weights, usually a nine–foot five–weight, because it forces me to practice with my usual gear and raises the level of difficulty a bit. Sometimes I relinquish and pull my favorite eight–foot four–weight out and go to work. It just depends on how rusty I am and how much work I'm willing to put in. Leader and tippet sizes may drop to the next lighter sizes, indicators go from plastic to yarn, and sealed reel drags usually turn into click and pawl drags. As far as fly choice, I usually throw the same flies I normally do on bigger water, but never discount any historical, seasonal, or conditional data.

If you're not on your knees on the bank trying to keep a low profile and hide from nervous fish, you'll probably find yourself in the drink tucked against the edge in cover, while trying to cast to a spot the size of a basketball. All the while, you're attempting to keep your casting strokes to a minimum so as not to spook fish with the flash of the fly rod. The ability to pick up line and quickly and softly replace it with minimum movement is an exciting challenge. Again, multiply this by fast, short drifts from inside a phone booth and you will be tested.

Bear in mind that stealth, soft presentations and not lining fish is not only critical on small water but translates to larger water as well. As a matter of fact, I'd say everything we will discuss for small water will easily apply to larger water. I was fishing with a couple of clients from St. Louis one summer. We started our day on the South Platte Dream Stream, which is certainly not "big" water, but isn't small water as I define it. We had a fine morning with both of these gentlemen catching some nice fish. Around noon that morning, the water suddenly turned to chocolate and lost all clarity, due to refurbishment work being completed with heavy equipment upstream. We ate lunch and zipped over to the Middle Fork of the South Platte, which I would consider small water. We continued with the same mini–rigs we were using on the Dream Stream, and after about a half hour of over–casting, being behind on most mends, and missing too many fish to count, one of my clients said, "Man, am I out of practice!"

Exactly. We get sloppy when we fish bigger water that absorbs our mistakes. My clients went from big beautiful casting loops to dartlike full casts and backhand water–loaded roll casts in a matter of minutes. The water–loaded roll cast is a must to master for all water, but especially small water. The key to the roll cast is to begin with the proper rod tip position, and follow it up with a downhill, straight–tip movement. Whether the fly rod tip is over your opposite shoulder or at a three–quarter angle on your rod side, the rod tip must be up and behind you enough to form a D–loop. The D–loop may be compromised or elongated when you are water loading, but the rod tip positioning must be accurate.

Mitch Meyer showing proper mechanics and positioning for using a D-Loop on small water.

The D–loop is the basis for this cast, and if you can't perform it on small water, you won't be able to perform it accurately on large water either, even when you have more line out to provide for additional fly line weight and more current to help with the water loading. Keep working on the roll cast until you can roll cast the small stuff all day without a second thought and great accuracy.

Just a bit more about the roll cast before we move on. Although you'll probably not need to use it on the small stuff, learning to perform a double roll cast is very important on anything from still to moving waters. Many situations on still or bigger streams or still water require longer casts without the luxury of room behind you for a backcast. The double roll solves this problem. All you do with the double roll is put one roll cast onto another. For example, you form a nice D-loop and roll out your first cast using the proper mechanics. Then immediately bring the fly rod back up and into roll cast position as you watch the location of the indicator, fly line butt or fly line where it connects with the water under the rod tip. The key with the second (or third) roll is to ensure that you anchor either the indicator or the fly line, or the fly line butt section, before you roll. By this I mean the object must be static, unmoving, or anchored to the water before you proceed to the roll. It only needs to be anchored for a heartbeat before you proceed to the next cast. Also, and this is critical, you must place the anchor within the length of the fly rod. So if the fly rod is a nine-footer, the indicator, line/water connection, or line butt must be anchored on the water surface within nine feet of you before you begin the next roll cast. This is easily practiced in your front yard.

Working Upstream

Whether you're roll casting or performing a full cast, you have to be able to work upstream in small water. Typically, fish that inhabit small water have to be on constant lookout for predation. When they do move into feeding lanes, you're most often relegated to upstream casting, in an attempt to fish without spooking them, as the slightest overhead movement will send them flashing for cover. Again, movement must be minimal, and casts must be precise and soft. The problem with upstream casting is that the fly line can spook the fish as it drifts over them. Even when throwing dry flies, your bugs may not spook fish, but the cast and the line may. Learning to angle your casts so as not to "line" the fish is a great skill to master. You can attempt to move quietly to one side or the other, in order to create an angle that prevents your line from going directly over feeding fish, while your bugs will follow a path directly over them.

Folks ask me a lot how do you control the speed of the drift that is coming right at you? The answer is quite simple but takes a bit of practice to master. Once you've laid the line upstream, it immediately begins to flow toward you. There are two critical elements here to take complete control of this drift, because it can get away from you quickly on water of any size.

The first rule is to keep your fly rod tip exactly where it was when your flies hit the water, which is usually around three o'clock out front of you. All too often, folks pick up the rod tip and pull the flies toward them the second the bugs hit the water. I'm not sure why, but I see this a bunch with inexperienced folks. Leave the fly rod flat to the water and immediately bring your hands together, with your nondominant hand holding onto the management loop. What you want to attain and maintain is a ninety-degree angle of fly line to the water. That's the second rule: preventing the fly line from looping under the rod tip, as you strip in line and raise the fly rod, keeping it *flat* to the water. If you are stripping the line and raising the fly rod too quickly, you won't have a ninety-degree angle and you will be pulling the flies. Of course, the faster the water, the faster you'll have to work.

In the picture, you'll notice a flat, low fly rod. The hands are working the fly rod and management loop together as the angler is able to keep his eyes glued to the indicator. You'll also notice the angler is inducing an upstream slack mend into the drift. Again, the keys to this very effective drift are to keep the rod tip low to the water, lift and strip during the drift, add upstream slack mends as needed, and maintain a ninety-degree angle between the rod tip and the fly line.

Upstream work can be very effective if all of the moving parts are in synchronization.

I use the tuck cast plenty to get my bugs down quickly. If you're nymphing small water, you're probably running long and lean. The long and lean nymph rig is a good choice, but casting it can be a nightmare on small water, because the indicator is far from the flies. This makes it difficult to judge lengths of casts. You may have your indicator hit well this side of the opposite bank, while your flies have found a nice home in the bushes. Also, given the minimum of five feet from the indicator to the top fly in your lean rig, the line and leader want to hit and roll out on the water surface well before your flies. This action immediately begins to pull at your flies, dragging them downstream, so you have to put a vigorous upstream mend in place. This mend has a good chance of spooking resident fish.

Notice that the flies are hitting the water well ahead of the indicator and line. This cast is a great tool anytime you need to hasten the flies sinking.

A tuck cast is designed to allow for your flies to strike the water before the rest of your line. I was doing this as a kid on high–country Arizona small water before I even knew it had a name. You can perform this cast from a full cast or roll cast, provided you have the proper cast mechanics. Simply stop the fly rod as you cast forward, at about a two–o'clock angle. Just as the line begins to straighten, move your rod hand as if you're using a bottle opener. This motion forces an abrupt downward movement of the fly rod tip, and accelerates the flies into a position to strike the water first. When the bugs hit first, this removes the need for a large initial mend in small and big water alike. The tuck cast will also save you many flies and many episodes of spooking fish with casting. The fewer flies you put in the bushes on the other bank, the fewer fish you spook retrieving them or shaking the bushes as you attempt to untangle. When you master the tuck cast, you'll be able to tuck your flies into a five–gallon bucket near the far bank, with the flies coming straight out of the sky. The benefits of a tuck cast are many.

The other cast I use is the reach cast. I'll use it on small and big water alike, but the benefits really shine on small water. Let's imagine you're fishing a small bend from a kneeling position, on your favorite small water. The water is moving from left to right as it transitions from tailout to a very short riffle, then immediately to a three–foot shelf in less than two feet of water. You can read the water easily, knowing the fish will be set up on the lower portion of the shelf. To make things easier, you can see three or four nice fish sitting right where there supposed to. Now in two feet of water, if you can see the fish, there's a good chance they can see you as well. Or at least see your fly rod flash, or line slap, or mend slap. There's a lot that can go wrong here.

The way I approach this is to set up downstream of the fish, probably on a knee to lower my profile. I'll then flip my line downstream and strip line until I am sure I have enough to cast the distance I need. I'll allow the downstream water current to load the fly rod. I can tell it's loaded if I see a slight bend in the rod caused by the current pulling on my fly line. At this point, I'm moving the fly rod slowly into the up position while keeping the water load intact. This is a very critical part of this entire process: move the fly rod too quickly into position and I can spook fish from the movement or lose the fly rod load, or both. I slow down here. Next, I perform my forward roll cast, and as my line begins to straighten and my rod tip is close to a three–o'clock angle, I move the rod tip "up and over" to my left. Basically, I am throwing in a reach mend to my cast. It's a beautiful thing to see as my pre–mended line lands on the water and begins its drift, without need for another mend, right toward my intended target.

Here the author demonstrates a reach cast. Notice that the line is fully mended up stream as the indicator makes contact with the water. This cast should be in your bag of tricks.

MEND MINDING

As you can figure, keeping mending to a minimum is a must on small water. I believe minimizing mending as much as possible translates well to big water, especially highly pressured water, but you can certainly get away with more movement on bigger water in most cases. My advice is, and it's worth repeating, learn to anticipate the next mend, never mend over fish, mend before your drift gets to the fish, and use pre–mend techniques like the reach and tuck casts as much as possible. In smaller water, you often need to work upstream, from below the fish; therefore, learning to cast upstream "pre–mended" can be a huge benefit. I like to throw a shock–absorber "S" mend into the cast when working upstream. This places a mend within the line, which allows the angler time before the pick–up begins, which slows the entire downstream drift as well, allowing droppers to reach proper depths.

All you do is mentally calculate the amount of line you will need to get your flies where you want them, strip out an extra four or five feet of line, depending on the original cast length, and then perform your upstream cast. As your cast straightens out, with the fly rod in the three–o'clock position, wiggle the rod tip side to side while allowing the extra slack you pulled to sift through your fingers and be added to the cast. This puts an S–shaped pre–mend all the way to your flies. You can also mend to your upstream cast by stripping the same amount of line as described, then making your cast without releasing additional line or wiggling the rod tip side-to-side. After the cast, lower your fly rod tip so it's slightly above the water surface, with a quick upward, forward, and side–to–side rod tip movement you release or throw the fly line up, out and away with enough force to force the line through the guides. This places the same "S" shaped mend as the cast, but be careful when you choose to use it: it does provide for much more movement on the water surface.

You can find a lot of cast techniques just surfing the internet, so they're readily available and not hard to find. Part of becoming a better angler faster is looking for other avenues for information. Small water will do that to a person. Whereas you can find much information on beautiful casts, you won't find nearly as much when it comes to the mend. I find that strange. I think the ability to mend is more important, if not more critical than the ability to cast. I hear folks saying all the time that if you can't cast well, you can't fly fish well. There's truth to that, but I'll take it a step farther and say that even if you're the most proficient fly caster around, if you can't mend, you still can't play. What's more important on small water, the ability to cast or the ability to mend? Chew on that for a minute. Yeah, I know how you're breaking this down: *If I can't cast, there's no need for a good mend; if I mend well, it doesn't help if I can't put the flies close to where I'm looking.* We don't need to come to consensus on this, but suffice it to say, both casting and mending are critical to success on small and big water, but mending, more so.

Small water inherently forces you to mend better. I go to a lot of fly fishing shows and expos. Someday, I'd like to see someone standing at the edge of a long casting pool, microphone attached, talking about the drift in moving water. It would be easy to make one of those casting pools have moving water. Again, too much emphasis is put on the cast. Guess that's because it sells fly rods, whereas mending sells . . . what? Small water makes you mend quickly and concisely, one of those casting pools could easily show the proper techniques and timing. Your timing has to be perfect, as does your use of the management loop. The management loop, which is formed from the loop between your fingers on the rod cork to the reel, is often misunderstood. The ten–percenters realize its value within the drift and understand it's there to only give and take away line in front of the reel. Your hands need to work in perfect unison as you add or subtract line from the drift. Your ability to mend is a direct correlation to how well you use the management loop. If you are having trouble getting complete mends, it's either in the mechanics of your mend or in your use of the loop.

Here's a way to diagnose some of your issues with mending. It's best if you do this while on the river. Lay out a nice upstream cast of at least two rod lengths, at about a forty–five–degree angle. Let the rig float about six feet. You should see the beginnings of a fair amount of drag being imparted onto the line with a fly line bulge forming downstream. Point right at the indicator, indicator fly, or dry fly on your rig and put in a large upstream mend. Focus on drawing a circle around the object you're mending to, in this case upstream. Did you mend all the way to the intended object? Did you pull the object out of the water? Did your mend only travel part way? If it was less than perfect, keep practicing until you get it where you want. You should strive for a complete mend, including the leader, to the intended object without applying drastic movement to the object (surface fly or indicator). Remember, you can only mend the line you can move off the water.

Now you come back to the river able to mend all the way to the object most times. Let's build an eight–foot management loop (four feet to a side) above the reel. Backing up here for a second: some folks are sticklers about which finger you use to make your loop at the cork. I happen to use a modified three–point grip on the rod cork, so my index finger is my "trigger" finger, which pinches cork and line when I set the hook.

All right, so you have this nice loop formed. Cast the same as before. Let it drift the same distance. Now mend to the object while letting out three feet of the management loop. This will cause the mile–marker–five folks issues, because it is counterintuitive. What usually happens if you're struggling with this is, the instant you throw in your slack mend, you stop the fly rod tip from continuing its swing downstream. Really focus on making that slack mend and continuing the fly rod on its path. Simply concentrate on pointing at your terminal surface fly or indicator the entire drift.

The slack mend is critical to most drifts. It either allows you to put a shock absorber into the fly line to slow a drift or adds line to the drift to ensure the drift stays in the same plane you originally placed it in. I can't beat this subject up enough. Adding and removing drift slack is critical to a sound drift.

Here's how to do the slack mend. You can practice in your yard, but let's break this down as if we're on the river. After the cast, slide your loop hand, which is your nondominant hand, down the loop about three feet. At the very beginning of the mend—and you should have these mechanics down—release control of the management loop with the trigger finger, but don't let go of the loop with your nondominant hand. Now, as the line is in the air in the mend, take your nondominant hand up to your trigger finger and "give" it the line to hold. After you hand it off, your nondominant hand slides back down the loop to a comfortable place. In essence, all you're doing is adding slack line to the mend. But to use the management loop properly, your hands have to work in unison. The last step of the process I outlined was moving your nondominant hand back down to the loop in a comfortable spot on the loop. This is because the management loop never stops. It's constantly in play, either taking line or adding line, and you can't properly mend if you can't handle the loop. If your hands work in unison, you will know it because you won't have to take your eyes off the terminal tackle as you mend. This is a huge skill that takes every angler to the next level.

Here are a couple more mending thoughts that are useful on small water and translate well to bigger water. Let's revisit the due–upstream cast and drift. You can use a reach mend within the cast upstream to keep your line off the fish. The only adjustment you need to make pre–cast is to add more line distance to your cast than you will need. The simple act of replacing your line right or left in the cast will eat up a lot of slack. Again, this cast will minimize the need for a mend and spook fewer fish, while showing the fish only the flies. Don't forget to keep your fly rod flat to the water and watch the ninety–degree loop angle under the rod tip.

Another great mend technique that I use and teach is the pile mend. I use this often when fishing slower water on the outside edge of faster water. What can happen then is that the faster water quickly pulls my flies out of the slower water and drags them downstream. I'll mainly use this when I am looking for only a short drift, and I can't comfortably get the fly line off the water using only the fly rod length, and more often than not, it's when I'm chucking dry flies. Put your flies on your intended target, then, without moving them, pile the fly line from the management loop to a spot that won't spook the fish, but allows for the faster water to carry it away as you strive for your short drift. You can also cast a pile of fly line into your cast by stopping the fly rod at roughly a two–o'clock angle on the forecast, and feathering out line from the management loop as you wag the fly rod tip in an up–and–down rod tip motion. If this is done correctly, this places a pile of fly line near, but not on, your target.

Pile mends can be used at any time within the drift to provide a shock absorber, of sorts, to assist slowing down the drift when your fly line is in faster water than your flies or indicator.

Small water and tight quarters usually mean you'll be trying to fish bank undercuts and bank edges that have a low canopy of branches protecting the fish. It's really difficult to get your flies under those branches to hungry fish at times. Here's an obscure, very easy technique. Place your cast on the far bank as close as you dare to the overhanging branches, or look for a foliage gap closely upstream of your intended drift to which you can safely cast. Once you're drifting, mend your fly line with slack into the seam that will carry your flies under the branches near the far bank, to your intended target fish. The trick here is to allow enough drift time for your flies to be sucked into the seam before you either re–mend to allow for drag or pick that line off the water. Works like a charm. With this skill, you'll quickly get to the stage where you can cast into one seam and mend into another naturally. When that happens, you've opened an entire new chapter in your fly fishing. Your ability to manipulate the drift in this manner, moving it from one seam to the next while adding or taking away slack, and you will begin to become elite.

Chris Grigsby using special mending techniques to fish under overhangs on this small stream.

Why didn't I get this detailed earlier in the book when I discussed mending? Because by now, if you've found a quarter mile of small water to fish, you've been able to see the holes in your mending game and you want to fix them. The importance of line and fly rod control is evident in obvious and obscure techniques. Finding small water to fly fish may have increased your motivation for improvement markedly and made these techniques really hit home.

Stacking one mend on top of another is also a great way to slow down the indicator, allowing your flies to get to depth, or providing a shock absorber, before you release them by picking up the line or mending into an adjacent moving seam. Stacking works well in big or small water, although most folks use it for larger bodies of water. All you're doing here is throwing one slack mend onto another quickly. This works great where you are fishing a slow seam out in front of you and have a much faster water seam in between you and your flies. Once your bugs are at depth, use a flat fly rod to quickly pull in the slack off the faster water as you raise your fly rod to at least head height. If you don't quickly get your fly line off the water after the fly's release, you'll get sucked into the fast water and will lose what you've worked so hard for. It's like taking only one aspirin for a headache. Right idea, but only halfway done. Most drifts require many different mends chained together while the management loop is taking and giving line. You then will need to mend accordingly to maintain proper drift speeds, and you will begin the drift with your flies at proper rig depth. Do it on small water, do it anywhere.

Around pockets where I find slow and fast water in close proximity, if I want to have my flies travel to a spot before the indicator arrives, I will use a pause and go mending technique. This is usually a close–proximity technique but can be easily employed out to a rod's length past the tip of your rod when you become proficient. The technique is exactly as it is named. You stop or pause your indicator long enough for your flies to travel downstream. Then you let it go, or release it, by mending into a seam and adding slack. The trick is in the timing. If you haven't done this type of mend, I recommend using a sighter leader to help you get the feel for it, as the sighter will help you track the direction of the flies as they travel downstream ahead of the indicator.

Remember, any time you stop the indicator or indicator bug on a dry–drop, your terminal flies move up to toward the surface. Stop the drift at the hinge point, and the sub–surface flies elevate. If you pause too long before releasing the indicator, your flies will simply be pulled up in the columns; if you don't pause long enough, you won't get your flies ahead of the indicator. Let's say you have a rock in front of you that creates a "glass" section of slow water below it, bordered by a fast water seam. There's a nice fish you've spotted in the lower part of the fast water seam, but the way it's situated, you can't place your flies and indicator into that seam together. You're going to have to put your flies in the fast seam and your indicator in the glass water below the rock.

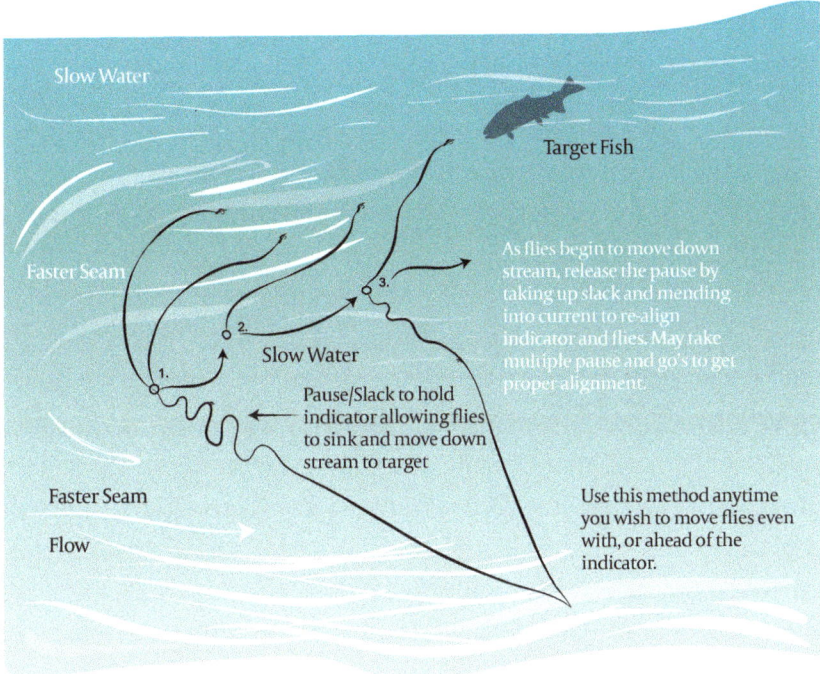

Without getting so close as to spook the fish, you need to cast your flies into the fast seam, while placing the indicator in the slow water. The indicator, or indicator fly, becomes a hub of sorts, as the flies rotate around it while they float downstream. If you did nothing here, your flies would swing uncontrolled around your indicator while they were forced up and out of proper depth. As the flies drop toward the bottom and are being carried downstream, you need to focus on the indicator. Just before the flies pull the indicator downstream, release it with a mend into the current while adding slack to the fly line. This releases the indicator or indicator fly to move along in the drift. After you do this a few times, you'll get the hang of it rather quickly.

Let's say you have found a super fish in highly pressured water that you are sure will bolt toward safety the instant it sees your indicator. You have to devise a way to show this fish only the flies with no hint of an indicator. Instead of removing the indicator and possibly losing drift consistency, apply the pause and go release to catch this fish. Set up upstream and out of view of this fish, build a big management loop, and place a cast well upstream of the target area. Pause the indicator by using pile mends while the flies hurry downstream. At the proper instant, release the indicator and apply any additional mends to smoothly and seamlessly continue the drift. This places your flies ahead of the indicator, but also allows for a drag–free drift, showing the fish only the flies. This method works wonderfully with dry fly and dry–drop rigs as well.

There is also a vertical pause mend that is incredibly effective, especially for long nymph drifts. The water at the surface and the water at the base are certainly moving at different speeds, as I've mentioned early on, but let physics state that the water at the base is travelling slower than the water at the surface, because of drag caused by the substrate compared to the drag caused by air. Without going into too much detail, let's assume the water at the base is moving about half the speed of the water at the surface. Therefore, simply by floating downstream, the leader and tippet between the flies and the indicator will begin to arc with the indicator out in front of the flies. Your indicator rarely shows this phenomenon, but it happens. This "micro–drag" is just enough to hamper a perfect drift, but not enough to show through the indicator dragging on the surface, but the fish see it.

Whether you can see it or not, it's not bad practice to place a pause mend into your longer drifts to combat unseen drag. This vertical pause mend is very effective for realigning the indicator to flies. I often witness a fish eat directly after this mend. To vertically pause mend, simply lift your rod tip to pause the indicator for a count of "one" and replace the indicator into the drift .Do this somewhere near the mid–point of your drift. This simple technique allows your flies to catch up to the indicator and erases the arc formed in the leader and tippet to allow for a more drag–free drift. Also, the simple actions of subtly speeding up, slowing down, and slightly lifting your flies can elicit vicious eats.

Small Water Techniques

Often times, when fly fishing small water, you'll be going after brook trout and brown trout. Although I know of some small waters that have nice rainbows, the majority of small waters I fish hold brookies and brownies. These predatorily voracious fish remain on the small side in Colorado, because most of our small streams have long winter seasons, keeping the fish usually between six and ten inches where I guide and fish. Every now and then, you'll hook something substantially larger, but it usually comes as a surprise unless you've spotted the fish previously. These fish are fun to chase, because they are often good surface feeders, enjoy chasing streamers, and continually compete for food, not to mention the game is many times faster than big water fishing. So typically, when working on your skills in small water, you are getting a lot of action with eager fish.

The real fun, once you've begun to master casting and mending techniques, comes when you begin to branch out into more obscure techniques which can certainly be applied to big water. I remember one day fishing a small Arizona stream on the White Mountain Apache Reservation near my home. I don't recall the name of it, but I could probably drive you right to it if pressed. There was a good caddis hatch that had been coming off for a while, the month was probably October, and the dry fly fishing was stellar. All of a sudden, the fish stopped taking my Elk Hair Caddis they had been eating regularly up to this point in a dead drift. The oddity was, they were still slapping the surface and munching away, just not eating my bug. I tried skating and skittering the fly across the surface, and even dropped a small Parachute Adams behind it, to no avail. I quit fishing for a while and just watched. After a while, it dawned on me what was happening. The fish were exclusively eating the egg–laying females as they dipped their abdomens in the water.

This motion, often called "dapping," is a very common way for some female species of caddis to lay eggs. It's a continuous up–and–

down motion of up to a foot or so off the water, with the female dapping the surface and depositing eggs. It was driving the trout crazy, and they had officially dialed into one stage of one bug in one spot. Try as I might, a dead drift would not work. I fished for a bit more, but finally left with my tail tucked firmly between my legs.

Years later, in college, I was reading a magazine article about fly fishing during a caddis hatch. I don't recall the author or even the magazine, but I nearly jumped out of my seat when I read about the egg–laying caddis behaviors and how to get those fish to eat your fly. I went to college in Nebraska, so I had to wait until the following fall before going home to try this new (to me) technique called dapping.

I was fishing a beautiful stretch of a small Arizona river that we always called Paradise, and it was mid–October during a fall college break. The caddis hatch that afternoon wasn't nearly as prolific as the year before, but there were more than a few trout eating my dry Elk Hair Caddis on the dead drift, skate, and swing. Just like before, the caddis females began dapping. I immediately went into action. I backed completely out of the water and stood back to observe for a bit. I noticed, several feet upstream a couple of waist–high thickly leafed bushes right next to a slow glide. The little browns were absolutely slapping the surface after the dappers. I snuck up and situated myself behind the cover, stripped out less than a foot of fly line and began to dap my fly just like the females. I had a blast and put many fish into the bag, even after the egg–laying was all but over, I continued to move fish in this manner.

Truth is, fish don't always eat dappers where you can dap right under your fly rod tip. On the Eagle River, this feeding frenzy sometimes takes place mid–river, two or three rod lengths away. When this happens, I have my clients over–mend to mimic the dapping behavior of the caddis. Simply cast into the seam with feeding fish, when you are over the target area, over–mend, meaning, place a hard and tight mend upstream. As the mend reaches your flies, it picks them up into a tight loop over the river, and then drops them back onto the surface. We will do this several times in a drift, and often, just after the fly comes makes contact with the surface, a splashy rise ensues. The mend, if done correctly, creates a long, tight corkscrew with the fly line and works like a charm mimicking dappers. Remember to show the fish only the flies.

Special Fish Holds

In earlier chapters, we talked in detail about reading the river horizontally and vertically. We mostly discussed easily recognizable river features. Small water makes you really concentrate when you read it, because of the nature of the quick transitions. You have to look for specialized features that hold fish. These areas are obscure but easily recognizable once you know what you're looking for and, as always, correlate to larger water. I am talking about bathtubs, sinks, back walls, and sleeper seams. The elite not only know how to find these features, but how to best fish them.

If you're having a so–so day on the river, and find a few sinks to fish, you can really improve it. If you're having a good day, finding and fishing sinks can take it from good to stellar. Sinks are features you have to look for. And once you find them, you have to design a plan of attack, because there's not just one way to fish sinks. You have to be flexible and versatile, knowing many techniques. You need the abilities to set up, cast, and supply short perfect drifts in sensitive areas.

Sinks are fish holding areas that are about the size and depth of a double kitchen sink. Often, they are surrounded by less than favorable holding water, or they are small areas tucked next to obstructions like rocks or logs.

An Eagle River, Colorado sink. Notice the entry and exit on the left side? Clients have caught and landed several from this sink.

I was walking the bank one day with clients in tow on the Eagle River. We trudged up the bank, rock hopping and walking on rock bars that extended well into the river. I saw a spot ahead and upstream that looked like it could hold fish. For some reason, I didn't pause to inspect it, but just walked right into it. I spooked a real nice rainbow out of that hold and proceeded to kick myself. A couple of days later, I was walking the same beat, and stopped short of the sink I had found. My client and I stayed in the brush while inspecting the hold. We couldn't see any inhabitant, but I wasn't convinced. We backed down the bank, dropped off the nymph rig, and picked up the mini–rig. The strategy was to move within twenty feet of the sink, cast into the upper perimeter as far as possible, and then work to pull off a perfect three–foot drift, showing any fish in the sink only the flies.

A beautiful eighteen–inch brown ate one of the droppers and proceeded to haul the mail through a fissure in the rocks we didn't notice, which took her directly into the main stem. We landed that fish downstream a bit and learned several valuable lessons. I have found and fished countless sinks since then: they all have the same few characteristics. Usually, a sink only holds one fish, it's not always the same fish, and it's nearly always a dominant fish. It has an entrance and an exit, and often those are the same path. I have found many sinks in low water conditions that are also prime lies for several trout in higher water conditions, but often lack the big bruisers you find in a low–water sink.

Typically, the best way to fish a sink is with an unobtrusive rig like a dry fly or mini–rig, as these tend not to spook fish as readily as an indicator rig. Sure, you can go long and lean under the indicator or remove the bobber altogether, which I've done on occasion, but running surface flies with or without droppers has been my best producer. Fish in sinks are there to eat. They are usually dominant loners intent on food; therefore, your setup and presentation is much more critical than the flies you are throwing. Usually, an off–angle upstream presentation is called for when fishing sinks. This keeps you downstream of the fish and helps hide your profile. Since most sinks I have found are less than a foot and a half deep, you can get fairly close, depending on your height, and still stay undetected. Minimize fly rod flash when casting. Less is more.

A bathtub is an area that is usually up to five feet deep, is bound on at least three sides by rocks or other obstructions and is less than two rod lengths long and one rod length wide. One of the perimeter definers is always the top or "faucet end" of the bathtub. The Eagle River is ripe with bathtubs, and I have had to figure out how to fish them over the years. The usual way to fish a bathtub is with a nymph rig. The trick is to get your flies down quickly and right over the head of the bathtub, get them to drift the bottom effectively, and lift them up along the back end of the tub. Fish will eat in any part of the run in a bathtub, but most strikes occur on the lift at the backend.

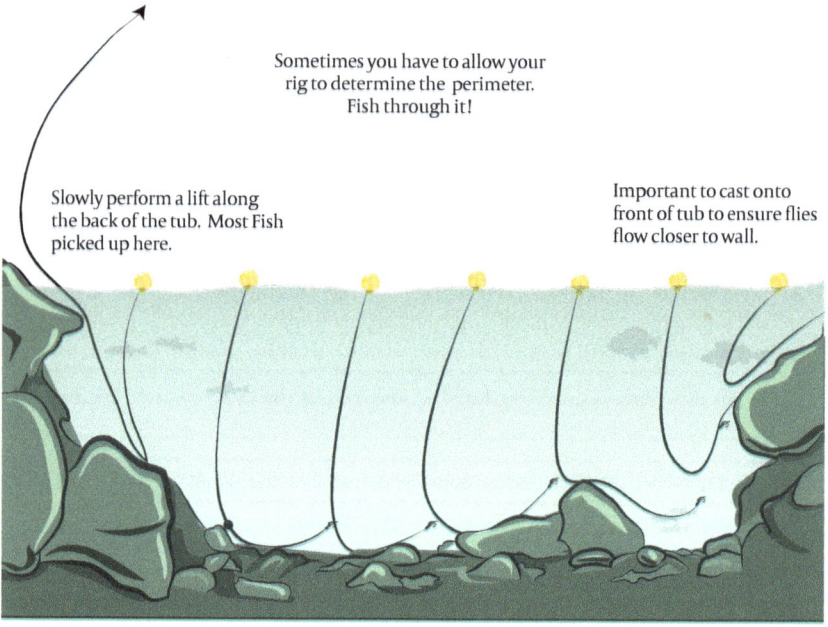

Sometimes you have to allow your rig to determine the perimeter. Fish through it!

Slowly perform a lift along the back of the tub. Most Fish picked up here.

Important to cast onto front of tub to ensure flies flow closer to wall.

Depending on the width of the bathtub, you want to work it near to far. It is critical to get your flies to cascade right down the front perimeter of the tub. You accomplish this by ensuring adequate split shot to indicator lengths, proper weight for sink rates, and casting the nymph rig flies well beyond and upstream of your top perimeter. Just like fishing a shelf, continue to cast sharp upstream angles and incrementally work your way downstream with casts until you are dropping the flies right down the chute behind the top boundary. Make sure your drift is well–mended. Don't begin your lift until your indicator is well over the lower perimeter. When I setup on a bathtub, I will setup on the lower quarter of the tub when possible. This pays huge dividends on the lift, because you are more "over the top" of the indicator for the lift, and this allows you to control the lift more effectively.

Nymph the entire tub, taking special care to make sure you are fishing the sides as well. Same theory holds here as fishing the top and bottom perimeters: keep fishing and allow your rig to define the perimeters incrementally. Often, you will find fish suspended in the columns in a bathtub, and you'll have to decide on a top–down or bottom–up approach. Watch how they're feeding. You may have to lift mid–drift, employ the mini–rig, or attempt to fish them bottom–up with additional tippet distance between the split shot and first dropper. Fishing bathtubs with clients is how I make a living on the Eagle River, and accounts for many fish caught. Fishing bathtubs on small water is an absolute blast, because you need to fish it as outlined, but have many other constraints looking you right in the face. Always remember to stay flexible and versatile and let the river and fish dictate your chosen methods.

Fishing back walls not only is fun, but can be very rewarding. Although most back walls are toward the end of a run, they can occur anywhere within one. Back walls are formed by obstructions, usually a line of rocks that perpendicularly cross all or a portion of a run. The most productive back walls are formed when walking–speed water bumps into a back wall, although back walls formed by faster water can be productive as well. Back walls are best fished with a lift or a swing technique; therefore, your physical setup is important.

A neat obscure backwall on the upper Arkansas River.
Anglers have picked up many nice fish here lifting the backwall.

If it's safe, I like to set up downstream of the back wall with my rod tip extending to the boundary. So when in position, I'm facing upstream, and my fly rod tip is directly over the backwall. In this way, I can work the portion above the back wall, and it sets me up perfectly for the ensuing lift. Because the lift is a critical part of this drift, look to throw rigs that will get your flies deep subsurface quickly to set you up for the lift. Believe it or not, one of my favorite techniques here is casting streamers above the back wall and lifting them along the wall. This is deadly in any size water, once you learn to meter the lift with experience. Double the streamers, adding a dropper eighteen to twenty inches below your initial streamer, for double the fun. This is a technique I use several times a year on small water Gore Creek near Vail, Colorado. It's very rewarding to have trout slam a streamer as you lift it under your fly rod tip on the backwall. Most times, I don't know who is more surprised at the hook–up: me, my client, or the fish.

Simply cast upstream, leaving your rod tip low over the water as you strip in line at the appropriate pace so as not to drag the rig too quickly. As you near the end of the drift, with your rod tip right on the wall, slowly lift the tip vertically. You'll often see the fish chase and eat your offering. You can do the same technique with a nymph rig or mini–rig. This is a deadly technique for several reasons, but mostly because it kicks a fish's greed reflex into high drive. They eat because the food may get away, and they are competing with other fish in the same position. It also mimics an insect emergence if done properly with the right flies.

If need be, you can also set up upstream of a back wall and swing or lift your flies as well. This is not nearly as productive, but is the next best way to fish a back wall when you can't get below it. Try to set up so you can nymph fish the seams and pockets above the wall and the end of your drift is a vertical lift along the wall. Experiment with your lift, because most often your indicator is slightly downstream of your flies, and, consequently, you have to allow your indicator to flow over the wall before lifting to ensure you're actually lifting your flies at the wall. I also enjoy swinging tandem streamers and soft hackles in front of back walls. Again, set up so your swing portion of the drift is at the end of your drift in front of the wall. Depending on water speeds, your cast may be up, across, or a quarter downstream. What you are striving for is good depth before you swing in front of the wall, because the calmer fish holding water is typically at grade directly in front of the back wall. Your flies need to get right into those calm spots perfectly. Feel free to twitch and strip the wet flies and streamers as needed. Have fun with this technique.

I mentioned previously that bathtubs are thick on the Eagle and I catch many fish in them. Once you know what you're looking for, they are easy to find, and become less obscure. The last feature I will talk about is never really as obvious as the others. I call this feature sleeper seams. Most folks walk by or through them on their way upstream. I have dozens of sleeper seams I have found over the years, on small and big waters alike, which I can hit when the day isn't going as well as planned. These seams have saved my bacon on several occasions.

I was fishing the South Platte in a snow storm this past winter. We were hooking a fish here and there, but we were going chunks of time between fish. I told my clients that we were going to go fish a long sleeper seam next to the road, but if they hooked up, I needed them to be very subtle about it and not broadcast the information. We crossed the river above the section of sleeper seams, got into position, and each laid a nice roll cast right into the sleeper. Without fanfare, they were both hooked up and fighting fish. Just then, I heard a car coming down the road. I didn't want anyone knowing about this sleeper, so I yelled, "Stick those rod tips in the water, boys, and look like you're not fighting fish!" Believe it or not, we landed both of those fish, and the motorist was none the wiser!

This fish came out of the high water sleeper seam that his nose is conveniently pointing to. Angler is Mark Kusner.

Sleeper seams are walking–speed water amidst the chaos. They usually occur in heavy riffles, exceedingly fast water, chaotic water, or water that you wouldn't feel comfortable wading. When looking for sleepers, look for small sections of "glass" within a very busy run. These are small pieces of calm amidst a lot of surface texture that looks unfishable and can occur anywhere within the run. My favorite sleepers occur at the end of a riffle section that cascades over a shelf. Again, these are spots most folks would walk right by, but if you stop and observe, you can usually find a sleeper or two. I have found more than a handful of sleepers by simply drifting a run. I've been surprised on more than one occasion as my indicator mysteriously slows in a run that is absolutely ripping. Rarely will you be dissatisfied when you find sleepers. Most often, the best methods to take advantage of a sleeper is to nymph or mini–rig it, but any method, if done correctly, will move fish.

Sleepers usually require short–line, high–stick techniques because the water around sleeper seams is traveling at a much faster rate than the sleeper seam itself. Long–line mending, although it can be done in some instances, is not the method of choice, simply because the faster water wants to rip your fly line downstream, ruining your drift. A shoulder–high, flat fly rod, also known as a high stick, with minimum line on the water, is the best way to fish sleepers amidst the chaos. I always look for a way to fish sleepers with upstream technique where safe, and in this case, you can use long–line upstream presentations to move many fish. Sleepers occur everywhere. The more you fish them, the less obscure they become, and the more fish you will catch. There's probably a few in your quarter mile.

Tie Your Own

I tied my first fly when I was nine years old at a fly fishing club in Tucson, Arizona. It was a wooly worm, tied on an old Thompson vice, and from that moment I was hooked. Tying your own flies, in my opinion, can hasten the fly fishing journey, can help you improve quickly. The combination of tying your own and fishing small water helps you because you can throw less than perfect bugs to less discerning fish.

If you don't have any tying gear and want to get into it, it's pretty much like any other new venture. Purchase what you can afford. Find yourself a mentor, club, social media group, or anything that clips the top off the learning curve. And tie. Not only is it satisfying to catch a fish on your own tie, but it was not by accident, and you've learned a lot more than you think. As you get into it, you begin to think about entomology and the classes and stages of bugs in the water. For example, you will learn the differences between nymphs, emergers, and pupae and how to tie them. Not only will you be learning about bugs and their stages, you'll also have to focus on how the fish feed on each different stage. Tying flies answers a lot of questions, and in no time, you'll become a rock–flipping fool.

Start with simpler patterns, tie them over and over, and then begin to use those techniques on other flies. It's a lot like your quarter mile of river: learn it well, and then apply it as you grow. As you become more proficient, you'll begin to tie two–handed, dial in fly proportions, and eventually get into designing your own patterns. All the elite fly fishers I know tie flies to some degree. They get it.

Getting to the next level as a fly fisher quickly is really nothing more than frame of mind and effort. It's ultimately something you have to do on your own. Each time you're ready to take the next step, you have to initiate it. Small water helps you get better quickly because it forces you to take several "next steps" at once. Small water never lies and is a great teacher.

The Dance

"ALL RIGHT, THAT looks good. Enjoy it: you don't know how long it's going to last. Give me a bit of an outside edge. Keep your feet, it's not safe to move. We'll fight from here." This is usually followed by me saying, "Stay in your house, match move for move, you're married to her, give and take, mostly give."

You may be wondering what in the heck I'm talking about. The above one-sided dialogue is a lot like you'd hear if I was guiding and you were standing nearby as I talked with my client while landing a fish. Landing fish is the final chapter in becoming an elite ten-percenter, and there are some obvious and obscure tactics needed whether you're landing an eight-inch brook trout or the fish of a lifetime.

Folks always refer to the "art of fly fishing." Although I partially agree with that phrasing, I see a ton of science permeating the sport. Hydrology, entomology, physics, and biology are just a few of the sciences that are encompassed. Those are the constants, or more dependable ways to delve into it. The sciences give us a chance for mastery, or at least a good place to start.

However, we can determine what flies will hatch at what temperatures and what flows through science, but when it comes to landing fish on a fly rod, the sport suddenly becomes an art. Sure, we can discuss the physics of fly rod angles, absorption rates, mass, and how to apply those concepts, but the fish see this differently. I can't predict what a fish may do when hooked. I can only react, and all the science in the world ain't going to help me if I can't keep up with the fish. Landing fish on a fly rod is an art, a beautiful art.

I've compiled all my statistics from last year on how we lost fish that were well hooked fairly, and I think you'll find the results compelling. First, let's talk about the fish's part in getting away after a solid hook–up, and what the statistics tell us. My records indicate that we lost a third of our fish in the past year on what the fish did during the fight. I'm referring to fish that swim right at you very quickly, fish that jump, "gator roll," run like heck, or take you right into an obstruction. You know, fish doing what Mama Nature calls for to cleanly escape. Although 34 percent of fish lost to fish behavior during the dance isn't terrible, there are more than a few strategies to help reduce that number.

Before we dig into those, let's look at the anglers' skill level when it comes to the numbers of fish lost due to the factors outlined above. Looking at fish that spit the hook on the jump—and I count when they hit the water on reentry too—46 percent of the fish lost this way were lost to inexperienced anglers, up to mile–marker–three folks. These anglers are anywhere from first–timers to folks that have been a couple of times. It's not surprising at all that they would lose fish to a jump. What's surprising is that the next most fish lost this way were lost to advanced anglers. These anglers, which fall in the seven and up mile markers, accounted for 38 percent of the losses on jumps. The last group, which accounted for 15 percent, were the intermediates, the mile–marker–four to –six folks.

Again, I'm a little surprised by those numbers, but I think there's a decent explanation. The advanced anglers simply hook more fish than the rest of the crowd, and when they lose a fish, it's typically not as much their error as the fish's athleticism. The intermediates appear to do fairly well when fish clear the water, and that's probably a function of their having experienced this maneuver before: they have an idea as to what to do as a countermove. Like I mentioned, I'm not surprised by the beginner numbers. It's expected, and they'll get it.

Fish have been jumping since they've been in water. I will see them jump for reasons other than being hooked, like when the females are attempting to loosen the eggs for spawn, when they are chasing adult dries, or when they are being chased subsurface by other fish or predators. When they are hooked and they jump, they are essentially placing a huge amount of pressure on the leader and tippets, because the majority of your line is still subsurface. The fly rod goes out of the equation and the pressure is instead applied directly to leader, tippet, and flies. About the only thing you can do when a fish jumps and you still have amounts of line underwater is to try to reduce the pressure by lowering the rod, pointing the rod tip at the fish while reaching toward the jumper.

Often, when bigger fish are hooked, the fish will take line, and when it jumps, your rod is pointing one way and the fish is jumping in another, causing a large half–mooned shape of line between you and the fish. Not much you can do here, but try to lift line off the water while "mending" line toward the fish, without giving too much slack or too much pressure. Yes, you've got them right where you want them. If the fish jumps, and you have the majority of your fly line out of the water, simply "bow to the fish" to release the majority of the tension created by the jump. Be careful to quickly and smoothly reapply rod pressure the instant the fish contacts the water.

Fish that "gator roll" are displaying an escape tactic. Most of the fish lost to rolling come from the one–to–three crowd with 47 percent, followed closely by the mile–marker–four–to–six crowd at 39 percent. The mile–marker–seven–to–ten group loses only 14 percent, even though they hook the majority of the fish. Gator rolling is when the fish gets downstream of you and begins to roll on the surface with its face toward you. It's caused by the angler allowing the fish time to get its head out of the water on a tight line and use the current to aggressively roll to either spit the fly or snap the line. This is completely avoidable if you act quickly and decisively.

It's called "the dance" for a reason. The angler must match the fish move for move. Gator rolling is a function of becoming static, frozen, usually in the last stages of the dance as the angler is trying to figure out how to land the catch. When you do it enough, you'll be able to anticipate the roll and make a pre–move adjustment. As a beginner or intermediate, you have to recognize it quickly, then act quicker. When the fish begins to gator roll, simply reach toward the fish and out to the side, usually the bank side, with a low, flat fly rod. This move reduces all that tension, allows the fish's head to go back underwater, and puts you back in charge. Once you're back in charge and the rolling has stopped, you can resume the fight. Each time the fish looks to gator roll, you quickly make the same move. This may happen a dozen times in one fight, and if you fall asleep one time, it can lead to a lost fish.

Jon Wright using the advantages of a low-bankside rod position to keep control of a large trout in small water.

Next, let's talk about those fish that just take off on beautiful runs. These are usually bigger, dominant fish, but I've seen some pretty athletic sixteen–inch fish get crossways in heavy current and put folks into backing in the blink of an eye. A robust 83 percent of the fish lost on runs were accounted for by the four–to–six–marker intermediate group. The beginners accounted for 15 percent and the advanced group 2 percent. I think those numbers are as accurate as they are easily explained. The advanced folks know how to set reel drag, to trust the reel and let it do its work, and to get proper rod angles while maintaining poise. The beginners tend to clamp down, which we will discuss later. The intermediates have the ability to hook bigger athletic fish, but not the poise to let the fight come to them and trust their equipment. In other words, they panic.

I'm asked all the time by intermediates, "Did I lose that fish because I was impatient?" My reply is usually, "No, patience is when you sit on the porch waiting for the mail; poise is patience under stress." We then discuss how to keep your hands away from the reel when the fish runs, how to leave the drag alone after we set it, how to ensure the drag is properly set, and how we're going to go look for another big one to fight. The other side of this coin is allowing slack to come between the angler and the fish. This is predominately a beginner issue: beginners account for about 50 percent, the intermediates for 39 percent, and the advanced anglers for 11 percent of fish lost because of slack. This is easily remedied as well.

The main reason for slack entering the equation is when fish swim at the angler and the angler fails to react or reacts too late. There is a very simple move to help prevent fish loss when they cruise to you, and it doesn't involve moving away from the fish. I have had dozens of clients over the years who, as they begin to lose tension, will attempt to walk away from the fish, and have then gone swimming. Yes, at times there is a need to physically move, but most often, all the angler needs to do is strip line as quickly as possible. If possible, it's nice to be able to reel in line to catch up to a fish, but that is the exception. Strip in line until you get that tension back into the rod, and then spool the line into the reel until you're back in control. Make sure you strip line below your rod hand, under the trigger finger grip on the line and the cork. This way, when the fish gives you a break and stops stripping line, you can pinch the line down on the cork to keep tension while you quickly spool up the line and get back on the reel.

Fish implicitly know where they live, and when you hook them, they love to show you all the nice rocks, root balls, and logs in their backyard. Losing fish to obstructions is going to happen; you only have so much control. Sometimes I will just look at a client and say, "Well, she got us. It was like having a knife at a gunfight." I know most of the obstructions fish like to use on my beats in different waters, and when I am fishing a new area, one of my pre-checks is to find where the hooked fish will try to go. There are ways to turn fish and apply more control than what most folks think, which we'll dig into in a bit, but fish are designed to get away. They're good at it. It's part of evolution. The advanced folks, according to my numbers, have lost the most fish to obstructions at 47 percent of the total, the intermediates lost 42 percent of them, and the beginners 11 percent.

I'm pretty sure there's a good explanation for the above numbers, and again I think it comes down to the advanced and intermediates hooking the vast majority of the big, dominant fish that eventually will have their way with them. These fish are harder to control and know right where to go to get rid of you. See what you have to look forward to, beginners?

Get in Your House

We're going to cover my other statistics later, but I think I've gotten your attention to the point that we need to talk about rod and body positioning while landing fish. Always good to take a break from reading statistics, so now let's get physical. I don't spend a bunch of time when talking to beginners and intermediates about landing fish before a trip on my bankside discussion. I am more concerned with getting my points about presentation, drift, and set hammered out, as landing fish is better explained on the river as it happens. You have to lose a few to truly get the hang of it. Explaining to someone how to land a fish is difficult, and most of what I tell them is out the door the minute they hook up. I'd much rather send them a few pictures and a written discussion about landing fish the night before or tell them a few basic ideas to help them out.

I will tell the inexperienced anglers, and here I'm lumping mile markers one to five together, that this is how I'd like the set, and this is the position I immediately want you to attempt to assume. When nymphing, I like a nice, low-to-the-water, downstream set, long and sweeping enough to straighten the line and pierce the fish's lip. This action is like the reverse of skipping a rock on water or the reverse of a tennis forehand. Set low and downstream to the side and bring your rod hand up to a shoulder–high position. The mini–rig, double dry, and skinny rig sets are all "lifts" over the downstream shoulder for the most part. Dry fly sets are a different breed, as you want to set against the fish. So, whichever direction the fish is going when it ate, you want to lift the opposite direction. Streamers are a strip set: as you strip line at the instant of a take, use your nondominant hand to strip the line back to your butt cheek on that side. Mind that you keep the rod tip down on this set, and only lift as the hook–up is secured.

The reason I took the time to discuss the set is because I feel it's actually part of landing fish more than it's part of the drift. The drift stops at the set, and it actually can have a direct impact on landing rates. The better the set, the better the hook–up, and the better chance the angler has of landing the fish. The ability to pierce the fish and move immediately into fighting position is simply, and somewhat obscurely, one move. I'm not interested in only pricking the fish: we want to break through. To do that, the set must be solid and the initial positioning perfect. So, in talking with the one–to–five crowd on the bank, pre–fishing, I will show the different sets and the immediate physical positioning. I want them to set, bring the reel over their rod–hand shoulder, reach up with the nondominant hand, spin the spool to take up the slack, point their rod elbow at the fish, and let go of the line. It should take less time to do this than it did for me to type it out. If at any time during the initial process, the fish runs at them, I have instructed them to strip in line until the fish stops and re–tensions. As soon as the fish reapplies tension, spool up the slack and get the fish back on the reel.

I call this position "your house." This is an athletic position with your rod hand even with and slightly above the shoulder at the outset, and your shoulders square to the fish. Think of a house or a box in front of you, as wide as your shoulders and extending from your waist to arm's length over your head. When in this house position, you're in more of a defensive posture. You will take this posture early in the fight while striving for control. From here, you can reel in short bursts, withstand runs, and strip quickly if the fish swims at you. I like the fish to be totally on the reel at this point, with the free hand ready to reel or strip; however, I have watched many elite anglers use their rod hand index finger to apply additional pressure to the line, with good results. These folks can do this after having put hours into fighting fish and getting to know their equipment.

After you withstand the initial phase of the fight, your house will immediately expand out to both sides, as far as you can reach. Now you can begin to go on the offensive, and with the added leverage out to both sides, you begin to manipulate and control the fish. Be ever mindful that the fish "always has another run," so don't get caught reeling or putting finger pressure on the line when the fish decides to run. Use your entire house to move and countermove the fish. The long angles provided by using the entire house greatly reduces the amount of pressure on lighter tippets, and gives you a shock absorber effect when the fish runs or head shakes.

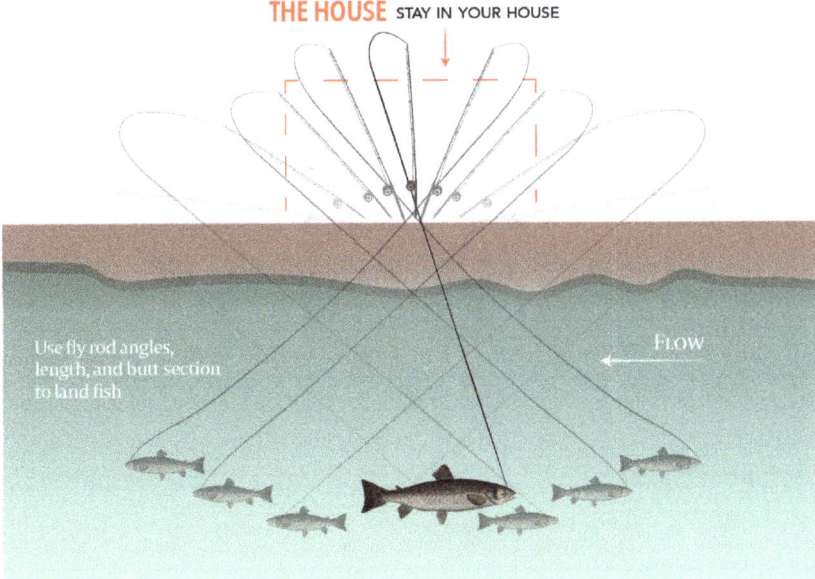

THE HOUSE STAY IN YOUR HOUSE

Use fly rod angles, length, and butt section to land fish

FLOW

Notice how I haven't said once to get the rod tip up? The only time you purposely get the rod tip up is for the brief instant after the set, but many times that's not even necessary. From there, I prefer to keep the rod tip away, if an up–angle is called for, then that's fine, but I cringe when I hear folks yell to one another, "Get that rod tip up!" Heck, when guiding one day on the Eagle River, near Gypsum, Colorado, I even had a homeowner yell that to one of my clients from his riverside deck.

Away from my body, out in front where I can see it, in a position from which I can quickly strip, reel, or get back into defensive house mode. It's an athletic position. Again, the rod tip may be up if fighting conditions call for it, but that's not something I say to clients during the battle, unless we need slightly more tension or the fish is about to be netted. More often than not, I'm asking for edges. "Give me an inside edge. Now a hard outside edge. She's gonna run, get back in your house!" Edges are simply hard angles with the fly rod, which is usually flat to the water, and extended toward the bank or toward the water. Edges control fish.

Edges can control a few factors that cause a lot of landing losses. First of all, a good edge is great for keeping fish out of obstructions, and it's great for stopping gator–rolling fish. Edges apply real pressure to the fish, not perceived pressure.

If you want to see what I'm talking about, try this experiment. Begin with a 33 ounce bottle of water. Tie your leader from an eight–and–a–half–or nine–foot rod to it just below the cap. A 4X leader is fine for this experiment. Lay the bottle on its side. Find a place with plenty of room, put out about ten feet of fly line, then lift the fly rod tip nice and high overhead while you attempt to upright the bottle. In this position, you have tension on the bottle, but you can't upright it. You may have to "reel down" as you attempt to lift the bottle upright to allow the strongest parts of the rod to do the work. Not only will you have to reel down to lift the bottle upright, but you will have to forcefully drop the rod butt to about chest high, and place the rod butt near vertical, before you lift. Now, lift the bottle to the upright position. At this point you are going on the offensive, but still haven't used all of your power.

Most folks think of landing big saltwater fish when they hear the term *reeling down,* but it's a very handy skill to have in fly fishing. We will dig into the reeling–down technique more later. Once the bottle is upright with your rod still over your head, feel how much pressure it would take to pick the bottle up off the ground. Now, engage the rod butt and apply an edge as you lay your fly rod out to your dominant side, give the bottle a good pull, and observe how easy it is to move it. I'm betting you could even cast it from this position—but don't do it, you may break your rod. At this point, you have achieved full pressure from the fly rod. The combination of a nice long lever, using the butt section of the rod, and appropriate angles goes a long way toward helping the mile–marker–one–to–five anglers get to the next level. Knowing what real pressure is proves paramount. Real pressure, when you engage the rod butt, controls the fish; perceived pressure, with a high static fly rod, allows the fish a chance to rest and prolongs the landing process. Not good.

Drag

Real pressure causes reel drag. I've got some pretty old reels that were built without any drag mechanisms. I love those old reels, but lost plenty of fish while growing up trying to use my palm on the reel to slow down a fish on a run. Palming a reel is a fine skill when used in conjunction with a smooth drag if you're good at it, but most folks aren't any more. Using the palm of your off–rod hand to meter out line to a running fish is not easy to master, as it is difficult to allow smooth acceleration of the reel as a fish runs. I have also lost my fair share of fish to trying to strip them in as opposed to putting them on the reel or "spool" them. With today's technology, I teach folks to use what's built into the reel as it comes out of the box. Not only do today's reels have great drag right out of the box, most have very easy spooling and large arbors that eat up line. It just doesn't make sense to me why one wouldn't take advantage of those qualities.

This brings us right to the "strippers vs. spoolers" debate. I really don't care how folks choose to land fish, but don't come crying to me after you've lost a great fish while refusing to put it on the reel. Big fish typically strip line until your management loop is gone and you're on the reel, but I still guide a few folks that refuse to use the reel to land the fish. I don't believe that pressure as "drag" applied by your hands is nearly as smooth and consistent as drag from a reel. I like my clients to hook up, get into the house position, and spool that line quickly. Many of today's reels are constructed so you can simply reach up with your off hand and spin the spool to take up the line. It's an easy transition and can be done without taking your focus off the fish, and many of today's reels have arbors so large that only a few fast turns collect the line.

Statistically, beginners are the ones losing the majority of fish during the transition, or the time putting the fish on the reel, at 71 percent of the total. Intermediates came in at 29 percent, and my statistics don't show it happening to a single advanced angler all last year. There's so much going on for a beginning and intermediate angler at the hook–up—there's a lot of moving parts—which makes it easy to see why they lose fish at this juncture. After a few fish, they begin to figure it out and put them on the reel quickly. Although sometimes I'll have to reach over and peel their fingers off the line and cork. Here's an interesting tidbit to go with my last sentence: of fish lost due to the angler clamping down on the line with the rod hand and putting inordinate pressure on the tippets, causing a snap–off or a pull–out, intermediate anglers did this the most at 59 percent. Beginners came in second at 41 percent and advanced tallied a zero. Again, this comes down to poise and proper positioning, time after time.

Setting your drag can be simple. Here's a quick way to set your drag using a partner. Strip out fly line to match the length of your fly rod. Hand the end of your fly line to your partner, and have them hold it firmly at chest level. Using an outside edge rod position, attain constant pressure on the rod, then give it short, quick tugs to simulate a fish's headshake. If your drag is set properly, the drag should give a few clicks on each tug. Too loose, and several clicks or free–spooling backlash will occur; too tight, and it won't click at all. Consider erring on the looser side for initial drag setting. You can always tighten it during the fight, and initial fish headshakes won't break you off. You can also use a scale to measure drag. The rule of thumb is to set the initial drag to roughly one–third your tippet breaking weight. Remember, if you get into a large fish that gets you near or into your backing, you need to reset your drag during the fight. The less line on the reel, the more you loosen your drag, because of the drag's "gear nature" and physics. As you begin to capture line back and put it back on the reel, give your drag a few clicks every so often to re–tighten.

Staying Married

There's a lot that can go wrong in the relationship between angler and fish; however, there are a few things the angler can do to avoid prolonging the relationship and instead bring it to a happy ending as quickly and smoothly as possible. When it comes to fly fishing, we aren't one–fish folks: we catch them and dump them quickly, always looking for the next hook–up. Remember, the relationship begins with the set, so why not properly set as much as possible throughout the drift? There's always something to set on, especially when nymphing, and the more experience you gain, the fewer eats you miss.

Once you get that good hook–up, and after you've survived the initial chaos and have settled into a good athletic landing position, you must be aware of rod angles and your surroundings. Now it's time to slow the game down mentally and bring forth your poise. This fish may be zipping in and around currents, stripping out line, jumping, and putting your tippet to the test, but you need to remain calm and quick. Think angles, and for heaven's sake, don't utter the "P" word. It's uncanny how many times folks lose a fish after they say, "I'd sure like to get a picture of this one." Just adds more pressure to the angler, and reduces poise.

In a perfect world, when you were fighting fish, they would always be at a ninety-degree angle to your fly rod, facing upstream in calm water. But that'd take the fun out of it: in fact, it would be downright boring. The more experience you cull, the more you look for a good fight, and to be honest, touching the fish becomes secondary to the battle. So whether you're looking for a battle or a nice picture, angles and movement are paramount.

The goal is to try to keep good lateral pressure on the fish. Side pressure helps keep the hook embedded and allows for more control over the fish than pressure you can exert to a fish at more than a ninety-degree angle to you. Look at it this way: I prefer to battle a fish that is upstream of me all the way down to right out in front of me but facing upstream. This is why taking in your surroundings is critical: you need to know early in the fight, or even before it begins, where the slack water is and what the safest route there is.

More often than not, the fish is not going to cooperate and stay in front or upstream of you for any length of time. The instant the fish gets below you past a ninety-degree angle, you need to make a move, any move. Let's assume, for the sake of discussion, that you have a clean and safe path downstream. In this scenario, you can move downstream to try to regain the ninety-degree angle or, better yet, get that fish somewhat upstream. When moving downstream like this, you will typically have your rod in a higher position to reduce tippet pressures, an outside edge, and you'll reel in quick bursts to collect line and keep the fish on the reel. The ability to move your feet while taking in line, giving line, and changing rod angles and heights, while keeping your eyes on your path, while anticipating the next move from the fish—it's an art. I have contended for a long time and will repeat: the most artistic part of fly fishing is the ability to land a fish. It is an unchoreographed, beautiful dance, and one wrong move sends your partner packing.

I always tell my clients that you move fish with the butt of the fly rod, and you rest or run with the use of the rod tip. The rod butt is that section from the reel up on single–handed rods. A simple way to think of the butt section is that it bends less than the rest of the rod and starts in the handle. Just like the experiment you did with the water bottle, when you have a high fly rod, you are allowing the rod to absorb the weight of the object or runs and headshakes from fish. There is most certainly a time and place for that rod position during the fight, but I find that many inexperienced anglers stay in that position too long and elongate the fight needlessly. Once you withstand a run, whether upstream or downstream, you have to develop the feel for when it's time to control the fish with the rod butt. Let's say you just withstood a solid run from the fish, and you're in great position in relation to the fish because you were able to move your feet. Now is time to put pressure from the rod butt on that fish! All too often I watch folks get control, then "bring the rod tip up" and allow the fish a chance to rest. That's not fair to the fish. Once you get the upper hand, seal the deal as soon as possible by reeling down on the fish to maximize the rod pressure. Reeling down is done with a vertical fly rod. The angler quickly reels in line while lowering the rod butt not the tip of the rod. This shortens the amount of line out and allows for solid rod butt pressures on the fish. Again, the rod is at an upward angle here to get the most from the rod butt physics. Think of the water bottle experiment and how this relates to rod butt pressures. Now the rod butt will be allowed to work as you push the fly reel down and toward the fish. The rod should be no higher than your head and in vertical position.

Lean into the rod as you drop the butt section and pressure it to a vertical position. This position applies maximum pressure to the fish, after you reel down to get the mechanical advantage.

I began to notice this technique while landing fish years ago, and wasn't sure why I was doing it. At first, I thought it was wrong, but I've seen hundreds of anglers do it since, and it makes sense to me. The fly rod is a class three lever, and it can impart or absorb force. The narrow tip is not designed to exert force as much as it is designed to release stored or loaded energy. The butt section, above the handle, is for power and control: you can use it to manipulate fish. I began to notice that when I needed to provide maximum force to a fish, I'd reel down, then the fly rod was pushed out in front, with the reel about chest high and the rod angle straight up or slightly angled back toward me. Then I noticed I was doing this while grabbing an edge too, while in fighting position. It was obvious: I had learned how to use the physics of the rod to my advantage while fighting fish. Hopefully, it is becoming clear that the dance is all about reaction, anticipation, and fly rod angles and levels, the command of which comes with time and practice.

Here's the other scenario when you hook a fish that runs downstream. Often, you can't move your feet. You have to fight from where you are and lose the luxury of moving downstream to keep the fish at a good lateral angle. This scenario takes all your rod positioning skills you have, plus an extra dose of poise. You hook up, the fish runs downstream, and then you're stuck, but have survived the initial chaos. What next? Your mission here is to somehow, through the fast and slow water, and in and around obstructions, bring this fish to the bag. At this point, you're not worried about getting the fish even with you; you realize you're going to have to land this fish at your feet on the downstream side. With the additional force applied to the line from the current on the fish and your line out on the water, you will probably fight with a slightly higher fly rod than when the fish is out front. You'll do this to take some pressure off the tippet as you really work that outside or bank side edge. Your fly rod may be extended as far as you can reach, low over the water, while pointed right at the bank. You'll take in line in short bursts, ever mindful of being off the reel if the fish runs or shakes its head. Yup, you are in charge, but precariously.

In that scenario, you won't be fighting off the butt until you have the upper hand. As always, and especially when you have a fish downstream of you, be careful not to pull as hard as the fish. If you're losing a lot of fish because they snap, come unbuttoned, or straighten hooks, you're probably applying too much pressure at the wrong times. If you notice the fly rod jerks up and behind you when you lose a fish, it's a sure sign you're horsing fish. Imagine you have a brick wall behind you as you're fighting fish, and your back's against it. Not only should you try not to hit that wall with your fly rod during the fight, but you certainly don't want wall contact from recoil if a fish comes off. Now, I know that there are unavoidable times when the fly rod needs to go behind you during the fight. That's fine, but it's not the desired position when you're trying to gain or keep control, and if it happens, try to get out of the position quickly.

Strip or Spool

I profess that folks should put the fish—any fish—on the reel when beginning to fly fish. As you gain experience and knowledge, you'll get to the point where you can strip in smaller fish, but make sure you have the skills and practice to make a smooth transition to the reel in case you hook a very large fish. Big fish expose your landing inadequacies. I see it happen consistently on the Eagle River. We will be moving fish in the eight-to-twelve-inch range, then, boom, we're hooked up to a twenty-inch fish. If you have a weakness, you'll be exposed. I'm talking about the little things, like bumping your jacket with the reel as the fish runs, or a spot on your fly line that catches on a guide, or a drag not set properly or is defective, or my favorite, which I see a lot, the angler misaligning the rod and reel to the fish. The rod and reel need to line up perfectly with your forearm and with the fly rod line guides. I'm always reaching up and aligning the reel with the angler's forearm. If it's not aligned upon a run there's a good chance of losing the fish, because it renders your drag much less than efficient.

Those are just a few negative obscurities that can cause you to lose and fish, especially big fish. There's infinitely more ways to lose a fish than there is to land one. The last step, sealing the deal, and moving a full mile marker closer, is the art of putting fish into the net. I have many clients that can catch fish all day, but when I put the net in their hand, they get nervous and struggle. There are a few "must-dos" when landing fish. First off, most of the time, you must have the fish's head up and have it moving or sliding toward you to put it in the net. The fish needs to keep moving or surfing until it's in the net, so you'll have to be able to use the fly rod butt correctly.

Second, you have to locate some slack or calmer water to try to surf the fish. Sometimes, if you're stuck where you can't move, the slack-surfing water is directly downstream of you. You've created it by blocking flow. As you battle the fish closer to you, watch for telltale signs that it is tiring. Look for it to gain elevation in the columns, get closer to the surface and list or roll, and lose interest in long runs. Without exhausting the fish, you need to move quickly when you see this behavior, while always remaining ready for another last–second short–burst run. Reel in to about eighteen inches of fly line out of the tip, lock the fly line between your index finger and rod cork, apply rod butt pressure as you continue to keep the fish's head up, and slide the fish on the surface past your net. I say slide the fish past your net, because I see the mile–marker–one–to–five folks lose many fish at the bag because they stop moving the fish as it nears the net, and instead stab at the fish with the net. Keep that fish moving.

When you are trying to land that tank you've hooked, try to do anything you can to land it from a position downstream of it. When clients hook a big one, we will strive to get and keep that fish upstream in preparation for landing it. I call this the steelhead move, which comes from landing steelhead in Alaska. Get the fish upstream of you as it tires, slide up downstream, behind it, and place your net two feet or so behind the tail. Simultaneously, lift the fish's head to turn it in the current, and drop the net into the water. Pull the fish all the way into the net, head first. Often, you may only get one shot at this, so you have to be smooth and decisive.

I was fishing the Eagle one fall, and my client hooked a very large brown trout while we were jigging streamers off the bottom with fiberglass rods. We worked to get the fish above us, which took some doing, and soon had a tired beast three feet upstream of me in slack water, ready for landing. My client was on my left and even with the fish, and I explained the steelhead move., The angler needs to commit to moving the fish: there's no room for indecision nor hesitation. In one move, he needed to lift the head and keep the rod moving in a high arc over my head and behind me. This slightly lifted the fish, turned it, and made it roll and swim right into my waiting net. Everything was going perfectly, the beast was halfway in my net, when suddenly my client quit moving the rod and we lost momentum. The fish furiously rolled in the net. I tried to lift the half of her I had, but she slipped out. I can still see that gorgeous rainbow swimming away. I was soaked and disappointed for my client, but at least I got my leech back. He knew it was his mistake, and I doubt he's ever repeated it since. By the way, he uttered the "P" word.

Crying Foul

It's going to happen even when you're fishing the horizontal and vertical grids perfectly: you will eventually foul-hook a fish. Seeing a fish foul-hooked anywhere but in the mouth is not only a lousy feeling, but it can prove harmful to fish. Anytime you make a fish work too hard during the fight, or damage that fish's mouth, eyes, fins, or protective slime, you can be severely shortening that fish's life. Folks that fish a lot can tell very quickly if a fish is foul-hooked just by the nature of the fight, so immediate action is necessary. If you hook a fish and can't seem to turn it although it's not very large, or the fish isn't tiring or you can't get its head up, you may be foul-hooked. If you're not sure, take another good look, and take action if you determine the fish to be foul-hooked.

If it's foul-hooked, your only consideration should be for the fish's well-being. We don't want to leave hardware in a fish, but we must put more pressure than usual while landing foul-hooked fish. This leads to more danger of snapping off tippet or leader, but it is necessary, because the fish is not as easily controlled as if it were mouth-hooked. If you don't control the head, you don't really have control. Most smaller foul-hooked fish, no matter where they are hooked on their body, can be brought to the bag quickly, while bigger fish take a fair amount of technique to land quickly without snapping off. So, if possible and if the smaller fish cooperates, reel the fish in quickly.

If you foul-hook a bigger fish around the face but not in the mouth, one that would give you a tussle even if mouth-hooked, you could be in for a struggle. Often, fish that are hooked under the jaw or on a pectoral fin offer special challenges because they can still maneuver at full speed and have control of their head. More often than not, if you're alone, you'll have to land them from slightly downstream of the fish as it rolls into your net. This usually means you've had to exhaust this fish, so take plenty of time before the release to ensure it's doing well. Keep an eye on it after release, and check the area a couple of times before moving to a new spot. If you're with a partner, double–team for a quick net job. You may have to "rodeo" the fish.

"Rodeoing" a foul–hooked fish is akin to being a calf roper, running down the rope to a calf before you toss and tie it. An angler can do a version of this move alone, but a true rodeo involves a net person. Basically, once the fish gets hung up in the current above or below the angler, the person doing the netting hustles down the line to scoop the fish. I perform this move countless times a season, not because I want to, because I need to. Fish hooked in the face and pectoral fins can prove fairly evasive, so it may take a few attempts to rodeo them. Fish hooked from the dorsal to the tail seem to always want to simply swim away from the angler and usually are much easier to run down the line and net. Tail–hooked fish are easy to rodeo even for the solo angler, because they often will hang up in current, on or near the surface, downstream of the angler. Reel quickly as you walk to the fish, and when you get close, stop reeling, use the butt of the rod to apply pressure toward you, and scoop the fish.

LET ME BE

Friend and fellow guide Levi Lambert asked if I was going to add anything in this book about removing hooks from landed fish. I think that's a great idea, and will do my best to cover the basics of hook removal. First, this job is always easier (and safer) if you pinch your barbs. It only takes a second, saves release time, and can help prevent damage to the fish. With smaller fish over which you have complete control, quickly bring them to you, skate them across the water head–up, and slide your non–rod hand down the leader and tippet until you find your fly. Grab the fly with fingers or hemostats and pluck it free without even taking the fish out of the drink.

Larger fish present more of a process because you now have a net involved. Once that fish is in the net, the clock starts ticking. The faster you can calm the fish, remove the hook, and get a picture, the better. Once I net a fish, the bag handle goes right between my legs to give me both hands free. Make sure you have the fish subsurface at this point. If I have to move to a safer spot to stand, the net stays low over the water, with the fish submerged if possible. Then the net goes between my legs. I wet both of my hands. Even if it's cold outside, I will remove hand coverings and wet both hands to prevent injury to the fish's protective coating. Now it's time to get to work, net secured and low over the water, hands wet and free.

Rarely will a fish just accept its fate and lay still. My job is to control the fish quickly with my left hand, as I slide my hand up to the pectoral fin area. I cradle the fish in my hand, being very careful not to squeeze around this area, because internal organ damage may occur and eventually kill the fish. Next, I need to lift the cradled fish slightly as you find the hook.

Levi suggests using the leader and tippet to guide your other hand down to the hook, which you will quickly seize, pinch, and pluck out the opposite direction it went in. He also suggests that if the fish is hooked in the maxilla, "or the long bars on the sides of the mouth," one should protect those by providing support to the area and not rip the hook out and damage the area, as they are susceptible to being torn off.

When I begin to remove a hook with the fish in the bag, I will often hold my breath. If the process is taking longer than normal, and I feel I need a breath, I'll put the fish back into the water. With all the movement and the need to talk with folks, any unhooking that takes over fifteen seconds is stopped and started over, after another fifteen-second rest. While unhooking, always keep the fish over the net and low over the water. This way, if you lose control of the fish, it will quickly land in the net and be submerged but still captured. I believe in having complete control of the release. Having them fall and flop into the water would be bad; flopping onto rocks, sand, mud, or snow would be worse.

I have no problem with folks taking pictures if they do it quickly and correctly. I've seen some pretty disturbing stuff over the years when it comes to getting pictures of fish. When with clients, I will put the net handle between their legs, get the fly rod to a place where it's out of the way, have them wet their hands, and, depending on the size of the fish, explain how to pick up and hold them. For bigger fish, I'll have them crab-claw the tail, just above the tail and below the adipose fin, with their thumb and index finger. Get a solid grip here as you lift the fish out of the net tail-first, while sliding your other hand under a spot between the fish's belly and pectoral fins. Hold them low to the water, and keep fingers out of the gills. Take a quick shot or two, and lower the fish into the drink or back into the net if you have a mess with rods and line preventing a clean release. Once all is calm, allow the fish to swim out of the net on its own.

Try to follow the handle-it-once-only "HIOO" rule for each step of the landing and release. I see a lot of people vigorously moving fish back and forth in the current as they release them. I prefer to find calmer, oxygenated water and simply hold the fish upright as it catches its breath. This can take place with the fish in or out of the net. Calmer, oxygenated water is often directly downstream of me or my client, caused by our bodies' obstruction to the current. Try not to put the fish right back to work fighting the current, and watch the fish until it's out of sight after the release.

Some of my best memories on the river have come from watching people land fish. I still get a kick out of landed fish and fish that get away. It's about the fight for me: the give and take (mostly give), and the punch–counterpunch with delicate tippets and small hooks. Just a couple of parting shots: pinch your barbs; don't put fish on rocks, grass, or snow; wet your hands before handling fish, and keep them wet. After all, we want to dance with these fish again.

The End or the Beginning?

I FIND THAT as I get older, my fly box organization and my fly patterns get simpler. I think this is a function of years on the water, detailed records, and a solid dose of stubbornness. I can tell you exactly what flies caught the majority of my fish last year (and the year before that), when and where I caught them, what rig I was using, and which species of fish were caught. Not bragging, but this is how things become simplified, and that can take you to the next level. I used to have to carry many different fly patterns and used many different rigs to chase trout, but years of information gathering has simplified things greatly. This simplification has allowed me the chance to move from mile marker to mile marker, because what used to be obscure is now obvious, as is the way to attack it. It's become not only simplified, but predictable and incredibly relaxing.

Scott Thompson enjoying the journey one early morning on the Colorado River

It has been my major goal in writing this book to make it all of those things for you, too. I'm trying to help anglers go to the next mile marker, and I believe the written word is a great way to get there. Of course, you have to add a healthy dose of on the river time to seal the deal, but anyone can go as far as they wish in this journey.

The ten-percenters are an elite group, but their status is achievable. You need to be honest in your appraisal of where you currently are, and dedicate plenty of time and energy to your pursuit. I've attempted to provide something for every skill level in the writing of this book, with a "pearl on every page." We've developed a common language and a common approach to aid in communication and educate those that didn't yet have that information. In developing a common language, we could then define your quarter mile of river in common terms, and allow for the testing of theory and the gaining of knowledge toward solid, elite angler fly fishing judgment.

Each experience you have fly fishing is added to that which is recognizable. It may take several instances to firmly plant it as such, but it all adds up. Soon, that which was once obscure begins to become readily identified as you continue to dig for information and put time in on the water. It's a fantastic journey as the angler begins to "see" that which is now obvious and that which was always invisible. The angler gets to the point that they can automatically decide whether to hit a run from top down or bottom up, and can" look" underwater by examining the water surface and letting their rig define your perimeters. It becomes automatic and systematic, fostering confidence. The exploitation of the horizontal and vertical grids is completely mastered, as is the ability to adhere to the fly fishing formula with solid technique. Once at this point in the journey, the angler begins to look for obscurities: the sinks, sleepers, and bathtubs that await exploitation.

In order to exploit the obscurities, one must be willing to take chances and risk not catching as many fish as you may be used to. As you delve into this, you will learn to use other techniques, materials and processes. This is a normal part of the journey, but to be honest, some folks never get there. The chances you take on the water today—trying a new casting, mending or drifting technique, or running only flies you tied—will pay huge dividends in the future. They put you on the fast track to quick improvement, not only because you are gaining skills, but you are consciously trying to get better. Conscious thought of cause and effect while on the river trumps numbers of fish any day, provided you tuck away that experience to someday make you better. Clients will ask me, "Duane, how many fish have I hooked?" to which I typically reply, "Not sure, but that's six great drifts in a row." In other words, let the game come to you, control what you can, and learn as you soak it all in.

There aren't any rules in fly fishing, only guidelines, and many of those are outdated. Find which feeding boxes the fish are in, and apply the fly fishing formula. Determine which bugs are hatching,

The Fish Revealed

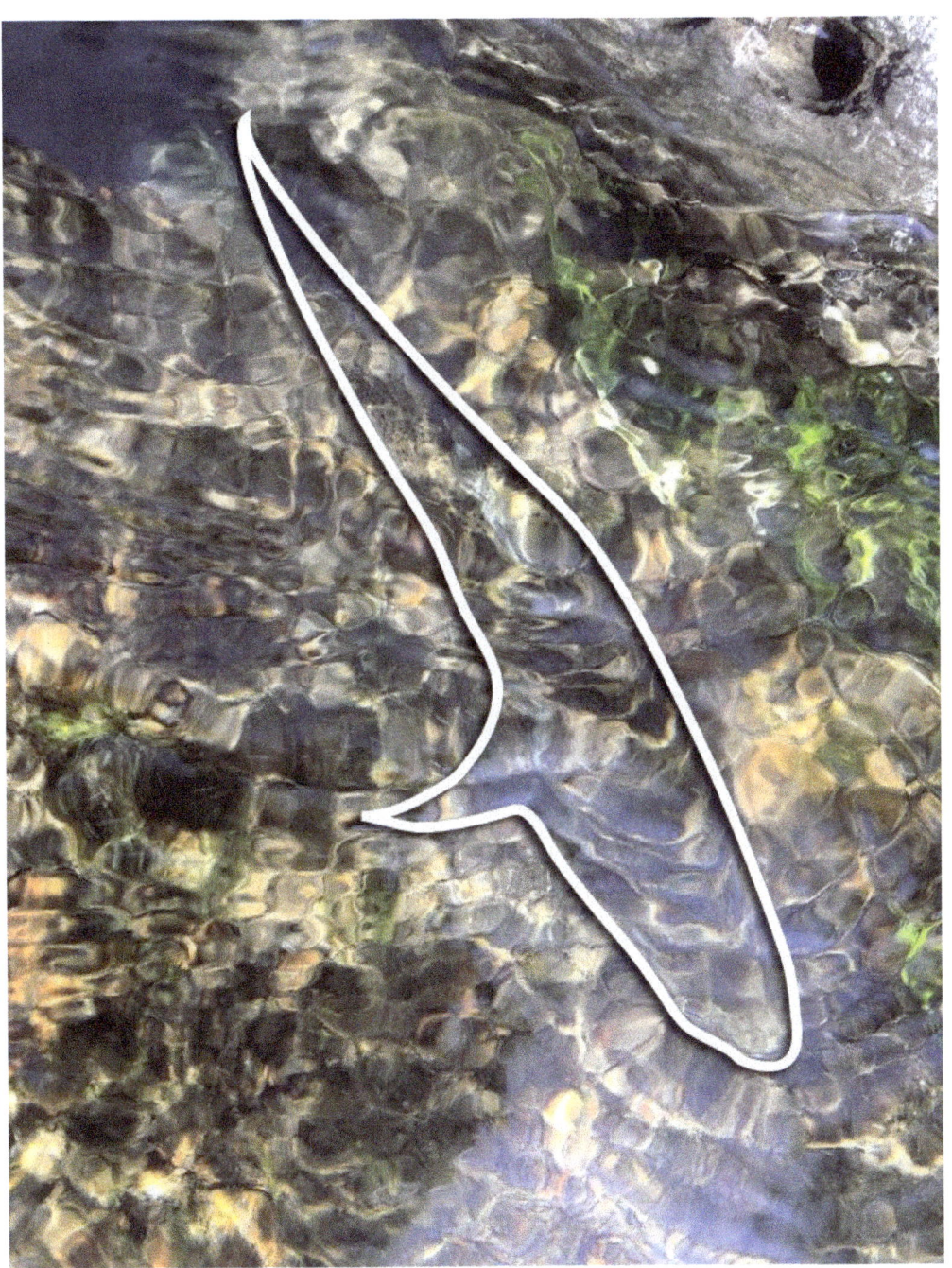

The simple act of seeing this previously is certainly going to help in locating it now. That's the premise of this book, things that weren't so obvious, are now, and things that were once obscure have become a lot clearer.

find the fish locations and how they're feeding, and reverse-engineer your rig to put your best flies, with your best drifts, in the best spots. You don't get sent to the penalty box for nymphing or stripping streamers after huge upstream casts. No one will chastise you if your first fly in your in–line nymph rig is not a big attractor fly, but a small size 22 midge larva. You don't always have to throw dry flies during a good hatch, or nymph when you aren't seeing fish noses. Just strive to put properly drifted presentations on a collision course with feeding fish. Heck, most of us have been doing that since childhood, but got caught up in rules of engagement. It's more than okay to lift, swing, or dap flies or use a sighter leader under an indicator. As long as it's legal and doesn't hurt the fish, put it in play.

I have tried to fill each paragraph here with as much useful information as possible. I've also attempted to speak clearly, conversationally, and succinctly, and break concepts and skills down into logical steps. My genuine hope is that this book helps you enjoy the journey as you get to the next fly fishing mile marker. There's really no luck in fly fishing if you can recognize the obvious and exploit the obscure. It's right there in front of you, hidden in plain view. Fear no water!

Acknowledgments

I have many to thank for contributing to this book. A heartfelt thank–you goes out to:

Levi Lambert	**Matt Redford**
Michael Faulkinbury	**Mark Kusner**
Gentry Smith	**Eric Smart**
Geo Schmidt	**Tera-Ann Smart**
Bob Streb	**John Frey**
Alan Peak	**Mike Connerley**
Tucker Bamford	**Neil Corvino**
Mandy Hertzfeld	**Mitch Meyer**
Scott Thompson	**Jon Wright**
Janet Redford	**Chris Grigsby**
The Redford Clan	**Joel B. Sharp**

www.ingramcontent.com/pod-product-compliance
Lightning Source LLC
Chambersburg PA
CBHW061758070526
44586CB00023B/2618